HOW TO DEAL WITH DIFFICULT PEOPLE

Powerful Tactics for Dealing With Difficult People

(The Art of Dealing With Difficult People - No More Conflict)

Joseph Wilson

Published By Jackson Denver

Joseph Wilson

All Rights Reserved

How to Deal With Difficult People: Powerful Tactics for Dealing With Difficult People (The Art of Dealing With Difficult People - No More Conflict)

ISBN 978-1-77485-251-4

All rights reserved. No part of this guide may be reproduced in any form without permission in writing from the publisher except in the case of brief quotations embodied in critical articles or reviews.

Legal & Disclaimer

The information contained in this book is not designed to replace or take the place of any form of medicine or professional medical advice. The information in this book has been provided for educational and entertainment purposes only.

The information contained in this book has been compiled from sources deemed reliable, and it is accurate to the best of the Author's knowledge; however, the Author cannot guarantee its accuracy and validity and cannot be held liable for any errors or omissions. Changes are periodically made to this book. You must consult your doctor or get professional medical advice before using any of the suggested remedies, techniques, or information in this book.

Upon using the information contained in this book, you agree to hold harmless the Author from and against any damages, costs, and expenses, including any legal fees potentially resulting from the application of any of the information provided by this guide. This disclaimer applies to any damages or injury caused by the use and application, whether directly or indirectly, of any advice or information presented, whether for breach of contract, tort, negligence, personal injury, criminal intent, or under any other cause of action.

You agree to accept all risks of using the information presented inside this book. You need to consult a professional medical practitioner in order to ensure you are both able and healthy enough to participate in this program.

Table of Contents

Introduction 1

Chapter 1: Find The Difficulty 3

Chapter 2: The Reasons Why Coping With Stress Is Crucial For Dealing With Difficult People 7

Chapter 3: Alter Your Way Of Interacting 11

Chapter 4: Further Effective Strategies To Deal With Disappointing People At Work 23

Chapter 5: We Are Not The A Party, We Are Unique 31

Chapter 6: How To Deal With An Obssy Person 37

Chapter 7: What To Do To Handle Difficult People At Work 41

Chapter 8: How To Handle Negative People 44

Chapter 9: Locate A Thread Common To All And Sew It Up! 48

Chapter 10: Resolving Conflicts 51

Chapter 11: The Gossip 70

Chapter 12: Strategies For Non-Confrontational Behavior To Handling Difficult People At Work 77

Chapter 13: Tips To Manage The Dominant, Pushy Persona Of Bully By Being Assertive 86

Chapter 14: Do Not Take It Personally ... 90

Chapter 15: What To Do To Deal With Difficult People In Public 99

Chapter 16: Enter Into Conversation.... 109

Chapter 17: Rebuilding An Adaptable Mindset 115

Chapter 18: Interacting With People Who Are Difficult To Talk To......................... 121

Chapter 19: The Power Of Words When Dealing With A Difficul Person 128

Chapter 20: The Guilt Tripper 136

Chapter 21: Discover To Effectively Communicate 150

Chapter 22: How To Manage An Uncomfortable Boss And Be Able To Keep Your Job 153

Chapter 23: Deal With The Difficult Person, And Use "I" Statements 157

Chapter 24: Discussion About Them 162

Chapter 25: Easy Rules Of Dealing With Difficult People 165

Chapter 26: How To Handle Employees Who Are Difficult To Deal With 169

Chapter 27: Different Types Of Difficult People.. 176

Conclusion 181

Introduction

Have you ever tried moving with someone, or even connect, but the person seems to be difficult to get on with?

Perhaps you have an employer or a superior in your job that make your working your life difficult sometimes?

Perhaps you know someone who almost all the time has a miscommunication or confusion and even after trying your efforts but nothing seems to work?

Finding a way to communicate with someone who is extremely difficult is exhausting and difficult, especially when it's an obligation. However, there are always many issues. If you have a desire there will always be an answer.

The process of dealing with someone who is difficult is now easy with the methods and steps outlined in this book.

The methods and steps described in this book have been proven and trusted techniques that have truly assisted and helped the author. This book is a compilation of knowledge from close associates too.

You will get a comprehensive understanding of how to handle anyone who is difficult, no matter who it is.

Chapter 1: Find The Difficulty

Do we not all have at the very least one person that we find difficult to manage? Someone who complains, lashes around, or and blows things off of the scale constantly looking for an excuse, someone who is blamed for the situation who's very existence is built on causing misery for all those around them? What do we do with this kind of person? It's not straightforward!

If the person you are talking to is an acquaintance or friend, you have the option of removing the individual from your lives. If however, this person is an acquaintance or a neighbor or even a coworker, what are you to do? It is imperative to figure out a way to manage the person. How do we accomplish this?

It's true that you cannot completely eliminate them out of your lives without lots of problems. If the person who is difficult for you is a member of the family such as a parent, or grandparent, you must figure out a way of getting in with them and keep peace within the family. For this type of person it could be slightly easier since you know why the person is difficult. People are difficult for numerous reasons, but two of the most frequent reasons are being unwell or unhappy. With family members it is easy to skip chapter 2.

If you live with a neighbor, your task isn't so simple. In the absence of moving out or waiting to see them go away and then you must discover a way to live with them. It's a good idea to find out what makes this person seem to be so difficult. You could consult a friend or a neighbor who knows the person. If you're not comfortable making this inquiry, or anyone you talk to doesn't have any knowledge about the person, then go to chapter 4.

If you work with a colleague who is difficult to work with, you'll have a job cut out for you. Being an uneasy person for every week for 40 hours can help you get rid of the last nerve you're clinging to. You must come up with a solution to get along with the person.

One of the factors that cause an individual to become difficult in their work is the level of stress they endure when they work for the business. If the employee is an employee and you are a boss, it is crucial to figure out a way to work and communicate with the person. There's not a amount you can do about the person other than to treat them with the respect your position demands. If you are the victim of harassment then you have the option of speaking with an HR professional or talking to an attorney when it's sexual harassment or emotional harassment or doing the next best thing, look for a new job or ask to be transferred to a different department. If you're prepared and willing to work with the person in question, go straight to Chapter 4 and kill the person with compassion.

If it is a colleague who is pulling your rope You can begin with identifying the reasons that make this person so difficult. Take a look at the stress levels this individual is experiencing at work. Take into consideration if the person has issues with their family members at home. This will not solve the issue of dealing with these issues but they could aid you in understanding why they're challenging, but not taking the situation personally. We are capable of taking a more when we know the circumstances of a person better. Always give someone confidence since you don't know the reason that makes this person unhappy. Does this stop them from being rude or demanding? It doesn't. It takes the burden away from you as the apple who caused the applecart to break.

Chapter 2: The Reasons Why Coping With Stress Is Crucial For Dealing With Difficult People

Nobody likes dealing with people who are difficult However, sometimes it is necessary. To manage difficult people, you have to control yourself and your stress levels first. If you work in high-stress work like retail, taking time to unwind and re-center themselves can provide emotional energy required to handle these types of people. If they don't spend time to refuel and recharge themselves could not be able to deal with stress-inducing situations of any kind in the same way they normally could.

The effects of Stress
Stress is a major issue that can have physical, mental and emotional effects. It cannot be completely eliminated since it's a normal reaction when faced with stressful situations encountered in our

daily lives. But, it can be managed by taking time to take a break and relax.

Effects of stress can be all-encompassing to a certain degree. Individuals working in stressful environments during the week are typically more stressed when they work on Thursdays than on Mondays. The weekend is a time to recover and rest which the less time-consuming, overnight break between workdays doesn't give.

Stress and emotional energy

Everybody has had a moment in their lives when they simply could not cope with a problem long enough. The reaction of the point of breaking point is dramatic, with yelling and crying, or even stomping off in a rage. Most of the time there isn't a specific circumstance that caused the individual to reach his breaking point. It's rather the level of emotional stress the person had at the time they fell into the incident.

People have more "fuses" when they're not under a lot of stress. Every person has their own individual way to manage emotional stressors and some are more comfortable with these than others. Anyone can enhance their ability to cope with stressful situations by actively reducing anxiety.

Reactions to the difficult People

The other reaction to the extreme "breaking point" crying or screaming is to stop. It is common when people find themselves in stressful situations in their own family or other aspects of their lives that they can't escape. The process of shutting down could lead to making bad decisions to please the person who is difficult. This is because the more healthy decision will require fighting and fighting takes energy.

Stress relief can help those in such situations to increase reserves and fight for their personal requirements to be satisfied. It can take more energy at first but could make a difference overall. When people feel like they are losing their energy may have to step away from the situation until they've replenished their batteries. They can then fight to protect their rights.

Relaxing Stress

Methods to relieve stress differ for every person. Whatever one person discovers to reduce their stress level could raise the stress levels of a different person. The most common activities people engage in to relieve stress are physical activity and social gatherings, peaceful time with family and friends and creative activities and more. In general, everything that makes people feel more relaxed after they're completed than when they started is a means to relieve stress.

If you are dealing with difficult individuals at work or at your home be conscious of your stress levels. If you notice that you're feeling excessive stress, get out of the situation. Seek help from a friend in dealing with the difficult person to ease your stress and restore your emotional energy. Finding peace within yourself will be your first move in being able to deal with difficult people.

Chapter 3: Alter Your Way Of Interacting

There are many causes for someone to be difficult to manage. One of the first things you must do prior to deciding to put the blame on someone or someone else is to consider your own actions and behavior.

Step 1: Study your role in the exchange.

Do you do something incorrect in any way?

Did she make a comment that hurts you Or are you reacting too much?

Do you experience this reaction often?

Are you a victim of a fault others often notice about you?

Did the person you spoke to touch on a sensitive subject that caused you to be angry?

Discuss the situation with someone you trust about the issuesuch as a coworker or a family member. Your emotions during situations can cloud your judgement. It's helpful to talk about the issue, then get an perspective on the situation. If you discover that the issue lies with you, the next step is to work on your own. Discover your weaknesses and work to combat them with strategies.

If you get angry or become emotional, there's the reason for this. Whatever others do your emotional reaction is entirely yours. You might think that other people are trying to hurt you or undermine your efforts. These negative thoughts could trigger a negative emotions that can cause a rage. If you look into the reasons behind your negative feelings, you might discover that you tend to become angry or defensive when believe you are being accused of some thing. One thing that people who are difficult do well is to bring people into difficult situations. If you recognize your weak point, change it into an optimistic one.

Consider, for instance, that you discover that you become defensive each time you feel somebody is judging you. Work on not getting defensive. Relax take a moment to think about what they said, and then clarify the situation when you're not certain. At this point, you'll be able relax and understand that the person who spoke to you wasn't accusing the person of not being diligent, rather rather asking you to update yourself on the task she had has assigned.

If you're not sure how to stop feeling negative or negatively, you should seek out someone to assist you in finding your solution. This could be a family member or a friend , or even a therapy. Make the commitment to change. It might be difficult and slow but recognizing the issue within your life is only half of the struggle. Change your habits and you'll be more satisfied because of it.

If you're unable to pinpoint the reason behind your self-defying behavior then the following step would be to speak to the other party who is at the center of the dispute.

Step 2: Ask questions and find the problem
When you next talk to someone who is difficult Make sure you are positive and

nice to them. Have a private conversation with them.

The first thing to do is find out the root of the conflict. is. Ask them what they are unhappy about you. What is the reason they are having difficult times with you? As an example,

This boss stifling perfectionist who scolds you for each tiny error you make. This can make you anxious and you're determined to solve the problem. You may request talks with her in the future whenever you can.

Ask her what you're doing wrong. She will tell you "You have made numerous mistakes, and you have graduated from college. You can't play with your friends".

You are sure you're doing your best to get this job. Then you think, "I have been doing my best in this job. But I get in early, quit late, and I quit when I am done with my task. So , what can I do to rectify this problem?"

Ask them questions to determine what is the issue. The reason behind their difficulty in their behavior is usually because they believe that you're not listening to them or don't value their suggestions, or other desire of theirs which isn't being met.

Beware: If you ask someone a direct question, you need to be prepared to hear about something negative happening to you. This could actually be the case. Sometimes, you'll have to accept that you could be the source of the source of the issue. If you say to them that you'd like to fix the problem but aren't willing to listen to the other side of the story, then you're far from getting the problem solved.

It's not easy to manage difficult people. It's a long and difficult process to change their behaviour. Once they believe that you're not a threat to them, they'll begin to appear more reasonable.

Let them know what you think of the way they behave. They may not be paying attention to the problem that their actions have caused you. They might not be aware that they're causing distress or pain. Sometimes, they might realize what they're doing, but decide to ignore or excuse. They may not even care. So how do you fix the problem?

Step 3: Be a great listener

People who are difficult often feel unsecure. They believe they aren't considered important and are only treated with respect. In most cases, all they need is someone to listen , without judgement. If you are able to observe without reactivity or getting emotionally engaged, then go for it. If, afterward, you believe that they're incorrect, then you do not have to believe their argument. It is not necessary to accept blame for something that's not your responsibility. Becoming a great listener should not mean giving the person who is difficult the right to vent his frustrations upon you.

Step 4: Take a deep breath

Be careful not to be quick to react when confronted with negative comments from the problematic person. Allow your emotions to calm to allow you to think clearly. There's a scientific explanation to do this.

In stressful situations in which emotions are high the part of the brain that deals with reasoning closes, leaving decision-making process to the primitive and emotional section of your brain which is inclined to flee or fight. The only thing that pops into your head is to harm them or to stay clear of them. Both of these methods don't work well.

Instead, take a deep breath take a deep breath, count backwards and do whatever is necessary to get your mind in order, then gather your thoughts before responding.

Be sure to talk in a place that is conducive the possibility of distraction. For instance,

If you're eating lunch, take one bite of your meal and chewing on it to help you relax.

If you're responding by email or text message ensure that you ask an outsider to look over your message objectively before you send your response.

Step 5: Put on their shoes

Yes, we'd all like to be able to live together and be content throughout our lives.

However, nobody is satisfied and content constantly. Be aware of how you are currently feeling. They may be experiencing something challenging. If someone seems less attentive, or naive or angry this could be due to the fact that they're going through difficult times.

If you consider yourself to be above others, then you are doing so

Immunizing yourself from understanding these emotions.

Believe that you are more superior than anyone else.

Perfectly secure and invulnerable

It is likely that you will alienate the person. It is possible to declare that you'd like to discuss the issue and address the problem that they face but you won't be able to assist them by displaying a negative attitude. You'll be unable to solve the problem they're facing by putting yourself as they do, put yourself in their shoes. See what they're thinking. Be aware that everyone is different and that not everyone has the same skills or views like you. You'll be able to improve your skills in dealing with these situations if you develop this mindset. For instance,

The person you work with is an anxious person. Learn to accept that. There might be a specific motive behind the behavior.

The boss you work for is an perfectionist. look for ways to view things in her manner.

When your friend vents her frustration on you. keep in mind that she is in a stressful circumstance that causes her to appear to be angry.

It is important to recognize that the reason why someone is having a difficult time can be related to more of their personal problems than what you did. You'll be able to remain positive when you realize the issue isn't yours to blame. Once you have that realization then your actions will come from a heart of kindness.

Step 6 To increase your tolerance

What other people do isn't something you are able to influence. If you recognize that their behavior is not your fault, you are able to decide how to respond. If you're working together or live together most likely, you'll be in constant contact with one others. If you see someone who exhibits a displeasure then you must develop a tolerance for the way they behave. Find ways to vent your frustration which aren't negative and can make the situation more difficult. Avoid being negatively influenced by their negative attitude.

There are numerous ways to do this.

Be aware that whenever they appear to be agitated the reason is that they're trying to find ways to vent their anger. It is possible to ask them what they would suggest to do without appearing offensive or sarcastic.

If they're trying to be difficult and asking unreasonable questions just deny the request. If required. Don't attempt to justify your position or blame others. If asked for the reason explain your reasoning clearly and avoid dragging you into a debate.

If they attempt to make a fuss of you, they'll try to make you feel down or make you feel bad about your work, Don't fall for the bait. Keep calm, listen to them, and tell them in clear terms what is acceptable for you and what's not.

For instance,

Your father scolds you for having let your education go in vain, after you quit your job to become an artist. The reason he's mad isn't because he believes you were wrong in letting your education go unnoticed

He's more concerned that it was a mistake to convince you to give your love of the arts and obtaining the engineering diploma.

You might be concerned that you won't be successful in your chosen field, as you can't imagine that it would happen.

You might be concerned that the public will not take this risk, and you'd be faced with lots of challenges.

Ask him what he'd prefer to have you enjoying what you enjoyed, or if he would rather see you miserable working in a position you hated.

Ask him if he believes in you to be a good person for yourself.

If he doesn't think you are right You can affirm that you are confident to do your best and close the conversation there.

There's no need to talk on and on You don't have to give the guy more ammunition to attack you with. Be still and let him end his with his rant.

If you follow these steps, you will be able to having a more positive interaction with the difficult people you'll meet. You've attempted everything to transform your response to someone who is difficult from a negative reaction to one that is positive.

Chapter 4: Further Effective Strategies To Deal With Disappointing People At Work

Now that you've completed your task in trying to find a non-confrontational way of approaching. However, your coworker who is difficult is still into your hair. It's time to gather your courage and engage in the initiative.

Talk to the person you have a disagreement with.

Engage with them in a private conversation. It is important to start your talk by making an "I" declaration instead of the "You" declaration. "You" statements can seem accusatory and the audience might think you're accusing him.

Example: Begin by saying: "I feel like there's been a little miscommunication between me and you."

Don't yell: "You said some really negative things about me to people."

Be sure to communicate your message in a clear manner. Tell your coworker what the consequences of his conduct on you. Maintain a friendly environment. There's a chance that the people you are dealing with have no idea of the impact their actions have on your life.

What can happen? The worst scenario is that the person might be aware of how they're affecting your life and might attempt to conceal the issue or even attempt to make a case for themselves through it. Unfortunately, there are people who simply don't care an inch when it comes to people with antisocial personality disorders. Whatever you decide to do, be sure that your discussion is constructive. Try to come to an agreement on positive actions that will allow both of you to take the next step.

Follow-up after the initial discussion.

After the initial discussion examine whether your coworker's behavior has changed or was it worse? Decide if you should have a follow-up conversation. Consider what if you talk to him again, would it benefit me? Decide if you want to investigate the issue by yourself. Are you ready to involve other people in the mix? Are you confident that your boss will help you should it becomes necessary to take the initiative of escalating the issue? However, you should try to keep the peace the longest time possible.

Conduct a public protest.

It's not as terrible as it sounds. It is possible to manage your employee's behaviour with a gentle humor or even a little humor. Sometimes, physical gestures that are overstated could be a way to respond. You're not instructed to show your coworker the finger. These physical gestures could come made in the form of saluting or placing your hand on your chest to show the sensation of being wounded. It is true that not everyone is competent enough to pull off these strategies of confrontation that are positive. If this is not your preference, then proceed to the next stage.

Involve others.

As mentioned earlier it is important to only include those who are impacted by the issue or who are able to resolve the issue. If you're sure you've done all you could have done now is the time to talk to your manager or HR manager. If you decide to do this be aware that you're escalating the problem. If you are speaking to your boss, be sure that you frame the issue not as an issue of interpersonal conflict rather as a problem that could have a significant impact on your job. Know exactly what your coworker who is causing you trouble is saying or doing.

Find other coworkers affected by the incident.

If more than one person is able to approach management with similar issues, the chance of being heard is increased. It may require a large group of people to convince your boss that the result of the behavior of the troublesome person is much greater and much more serious than it appears. However, it is important to be careful when you do this. If handled improperly it could appear as if you've gathered a group of colleagues to band together on one worker.

If none of these methods succeed, then...

Perhaps it's the time to return to non-confrontational strategies. Reduce the access of the difficult coworker to you. You should only work on projects that have nothing to do with be related to that employee. You can simply avoid your troublesome coworker, but do not let this avoidance hinder your progress in your career. You can also decide to change jobs to a better job within the company.

How to handle a confrontation

The issue with not being able to face an unpopular colleague is that you are left making up imaginary conflicts in your head. Maybe you lay in bed at night and play conversations with your coworker whom you're unhappy with. The problem is that you're permitting the angry coworker to impact your work but also your personal life too. Stress caused through these conversations could affect the health of your body and personal relationships. If a coworker who is difficult to work with causes you to sleep and toss in the night, it's time for a serious confrontation.

Start by stating the issue in the form of a single (or several) non-aggressive statements that are based on the facts.

For example, if would like to challenge a coworker for taking all the credit for a task which you worked on together, don't start with: "Hey, you stole all the credit from that Waverly account!" Instead, say something like: "It looked like I did not have any part in this Waverly account. My name didn't appear on the account."

Note that even though this method began by making the "I" statement but it's not an "I feel" statement, and therefore, it can't be interpreted as an expression of emotion. Be aware that the factual statements are essential. This way, your hard-working coworker will have a difficult time arguing with you.

Make your first statement, and then put it down.

It may be appealing to continue talking and let go of all your frustrations at once but you must be careful and let your coworker who is difficult to react. There is a strong desire to justify your original claim with a more convincing argument however, there's no need to defend yourself. It could be that you feel you already know the way the other person is likely to respond, the urge to speak more. But remember that this conversation is meant to find a solution and not to vent your frustration. Therefore, you should state your facts-based, non-emotional issue and wait for the other worker to respond.

Avoid arguing.

As mentioned earlier, disputes aren't always required to end in a tense conflict. Actually, this conversation is intended for constructive discussion. Take note of what your coworker is saying. Sometimes, there is no need to blame anyone else for something. Sometimes, it's not required to establish who is right and who isn't.

Focus on the issue at hand.

Before you engage in the conflict Prior to the confrontation, decide on the resolution you want to achieve. The type of resolution you are seeking will allow you to determine the way you intend to start the discussion and how you intend to start the discussion. There are only two options that this could go: either the other person will either agree with your position or they will not. When you confront a coworker with an accusatory tone and his response will appear to be defensive. This is why you must avoid becoming involved in an argument or arguing. Keep your focus on the issue at hand. Your colleague can effortlessly worm away from the conversation by redirecting the conversation in a different direction. Be careful not to get distracted by any other issues that could be discovered in the course of your conversation. At the end of the day, keep in mind that you're trying for a way to compromise and not choose a battle.

Chapter 5: We Are Not The A Party, We Are Unique

There are certain aspects of life that need to be considered. If one wants to be a king on earth, especially in the realm of socialization and other areas There are certain truths that are undisputed about life that one should be aware of.

We will not be able to examine all of these aspects, however, those that relate to the theme of the book will be highlighted to provide a clear understanding. What do these facts mean?

The UNIQUENESS OF EVERYONE

You should be able to recognize that there are no two people who are identical. The fact that we are all unique and distinct makes us different and demonstrates that we are not identical.

The thumbprint technology and DNA have proven this beyond doubt or debate. It is impossible that that two individuals could be identical. Even so-called twins have distinct personality traits. This makes them completely distinct, no matter the resemblance in height or facial features.

It is essential to comprehend the fact that it is impossible for in which a person could be compared to anyone. You must be able to realize that it is essential to recognize the individuality of all people. If you don't, you could be faced with issues of fighting, keeping malice in check or problems of miscommunication.

The present life is a result of a previous event.

The reason that a lot of people are in the current state they are is due to their previous lives. Even you. A person who is difficult or who has a personality defect may have had to endure some unpleasant incidents or received negative punishment from certain people. They may have reacted negatively, harden their hearts or changed their views about people.

The difficulty or the inability to comprehend could result from a breakup or bad situations, breaking of trust, loyalty, difficulties, accidents or betrayed. It could be due to any of the following.

A boss who is difficult might have learned lessons painfully. He could have been over-trusting and been manipulated or was easy to handle and accepted as a given. If you were in the position who was trusted, you would not want your business to shut down.

The events of yesterday could have an impact on today's events, whether in a positive way or not.

The Environment plays a bigger Rolle in the making of EVERYBODY

It is possible that the environment will not have an effect positive or negative on the development of a child or an adult of a certain age.

The society, the educational level of people, the ways of expression, ethics in communication social behaviour and more are the main ingredients that make the character of a child, or anyone else.

You shouldn't expect someone who's lived in the midst of hostile individuals or disloyal ones to build confidence in someone they have recently met from a different region. This isn't possible.

A girl or boy who has grown in the face of players and cheaters will find it difficult to believe that his heart is true or trust is secure with someone who is not familiar with him.

A woman who is the victim of rape shouldn't simply trust anyone, regardless of how nice the guy may appear to be on the surface.

If you are able to comprehend this you'll be able to improve your methods of dealing with people of different backgrounds.

The power of understanding

Understanding is extremely powerful. Knowing helps one remain in control of every situation no whatever. To handle different kinds of people, you have master the art of understanding. If you're unable to connect with people by placing your self in the shoes of others or observing things in a different way then you'll have issues with being social. Even if they're your children.

The ability to understand has many benefits. These advantages are private or not.

People will start to view yourself as someone that is able to provide advice and can be trusted.

Don't stress yourself out over unimportant concerns.

You'll have total control of your attitude and temperament.

You'll be able to be able to see and comprehend people as they truly are.

People aren't likely to gossip about your name and, if someone does try to criticize the person you are, that will be brought to your ears by those who have developed an interest in you without your asking for it.

People will be able speak and open their thoughts to you. Even the most difficult people. I've seen a scenario when a boos which appears to be tough in the public's eyes was taken by one of his colleagues as friend. Not just as an acquaintance but also someone who he shares his most intimate secrets to. The person in question has to have been closely watched by his supervisor to have an understanding of the spirit.

The last but certainly not the least you'll make many friends and fewer enemies.

Chapter 6: How To Deal With An Obssy Person

Being around bossy people is sure to ruin your life If you allow them to. It's it's one thing to get involved with someone who is manipulative, and the other aspect to allow her to influence you. The majority of people don't realize that they're being controlled and most of the time they'll get injured if you inform them. There are a variety of methods of dealing with The Manipulator and here are some suggestions to test.

1. Try humor

The most effective method to show your disdain for someone's egoism is to utter half-truth jokes. If she asks you to take action, you can say "When was the last time you became my mother?" Or if she is actually your mom, you could tell her, "Mom, the last time I saw the doctor's office, he said my brain was working properly." Be sure to keep things light and humorous if you wish to avoid any miscommunications or arguments.

2. Learn to say"no"

If your humor isn't able to take it, maybe the best option is to be able to say"no!. Do not immediately say "yes" to anyone who wants to tell you what they would like you to do. You must deny the suggestion in the most courteous manner as you can, but don't apologize for your refusal. You could say, "I don't agree with the suggestion at this point, and I have a different idea to think of that I'd like you to consider." Most of the time the bossy person will see that you're incapable of managing things by yourself, which is why she will always give you advice or making demands. If you constantly demonstrate to her that you are a person with your own set of rules and that you stand to those values and beliefs, she'll be shocked and start to respect your choices when it is time.

3. Don't give in to arguments

If you do not say yes the chances are that she'll be defensive and try to justify her reasons. All she wants is your best interest and believes that you can't take it on by yourself. Simply remain silent. When she's finished speaking to you, look her straight in the eye and ask her to refrain again. If she is not careful, she may make a noise and attempt to get into fighting. Do not give in to her demands and refrain from screaming at her. Keep your distance and display by your body and facial expressions that you are firmly committed to your choice.

4. Be simple

Sometimes, it is necessary to be direct and tell the person you are doing something wrong. This must be done in a manner that is appropriate however. Don't make someone look embarrassing in front of others such as. Don't discuss her manipulative behavior as soon as you notice that she's not in a good mood. It is best to discuss this in a private setting so that she'll realize that you aren't pursuing negative motives. Sometimes, the ideas of bossy people are accurate and sensible. However, it is the way they communicate their ideas and their expectations regarding them that make their suggestions unprofessional. You could tell her that your ideas are brilliant however, you are in awe of how she treats you.

5. Make sure you're an easy-going person.

Finally, look at your people likes. Do you feel good whenever you make someone satisfied? Are you someone who constantly requires approval from others to begin doing something? Are you unsure of your own choices, so you seek out opinions of others constantly? Do you believe that everyone is agreeing with you in complete blindness to avoid disputes or conflicts? If you're doing these things then you could be an ego-driven person which is the reason why you attract rude people to your life. Increase your self-confidence through your own personal growth. Recognize that you cannot be the perfect person for everyone, and you won't be able to satisfy all people. If you don't take care of yourself, people are going to be taking advantage of you every day.

Chapter 7: What To Do To Handle Difficult People At Work

In our work environment, we strive to keep a healthy working relationship with our colleagues in order to create a conducive environment for working. Our outputs are a reflection of the relationships we share with the people we work with, particularly in the case of team-based work.

Try to imagine yourself as they are

Each person has his own personal bundle of responsibilities with stressors, problems and obligations. Although we attempt to keep our personal lives distinct from work the reality is that they are a an integral part of us.

Therefore, try to take on that of your colleague. Knowing their position and situation can help you comprehend the actions they take. It could be that she is a sole mother to a baby that has special needs. He could be the breadwinner, as the oldest son who must raise funds for his father's care. This could test your patience and bring back respect for the person they are.

Ask for opinions of other people

Discuss the issue with colleagues in your work. Select two to three individuals whom you feel are honest and fair. If you can, talk to people who have been around the individual for a lengthy period of time. Also, talk to the employees who have worked with them for a while.

Make sure that other people have similar observations to those you do. There's always the chance that you're not the only one who believes this way. If that's the case, seek for suggestions from other people to help you beat this stigma against your colleague.

If they're having similar observations to yours like you do, talk with them about the best way to manage the situation.

Chat with them in private

A few people aren't aware of their flaws or they are having a difficult time dealing with them. It is an immense favor to let them know what other people have noticed and how they feel about them. Instead of discussing him with your coworkers It would be more beneficial to talk with the person in question to discuss the issue.

Choose a time that is relaxed and unoccupied and then invite him to talk in a private manner. Be sure to clearly explain the situation so that he can understand that this isn't an issue of personal attack. Make it clear that you are there to assist him.

Keep the "work exclusively" relationship

The standard is professionalism. If you don't come to the same level of understanding with your counterparts, it's totally acceptable. Do not try to force friendship on them. Be aware you are, at the bottom of it all they are the people whom you share a workspace with. The most important aspect of your relationship is the capacity to perform the task well and to meet deadlines.

Maintain your professional and cool. Don't let your personal opinion interfere with your work. Don't take anything personally.

Chapter 8: How To Handle Negative People

If you are with someone who is negative, it can be a problem. They continually complain about all the happenings within their life, including their relationships with their spouses as well as their children, jobs and health, the other people, and the happenings in the world today. They're unsure and think that nothing good ever going to occur. Even if you only talk for a short time it is possible to be influenced by the negativity semblance and it could last for hours before it wears off. If you are unable to completely stay clear of those who are such as The Pessimist and The Pessimist, here are some suggestions for dealing with these people.

1. Avoid engaging in negativity

People who are negative always focus on the negatives and ignore the positives. They also tend to making up stories about their concerns and problems that could make their situation more severe than it actually is. Pay attention to these signs and be conscious. Sure, you can offer an ear to listen as they are close friends, or even aid them in case they require help However, don't make their troubles your own. If she complains about the same thing time and time again each when you speak to one another, offer a sly smile or simply give an "okay" to her. If she is talking about something positive, you should respond with enthusiasm and approval. In this way, she will understand that you shouldn't get involved in her negativity.

2. As short a time as you can

Another suggestion is to be aware of how much time you spend with people who are negative to you. The most well-known Jim Rohn quote states "You have the status of being average among five people who you have the highest time spent together." It means spending time with certain types of people will directly impact the person you become. It is possible to entertain people who are negative for a brief moment however, you should avoid being with them for as far as is possible.

3. Do not talk to a group.

Most people who are negative prefer to talk about their negative thoughts when they are in a one-on-one conversation. If you're able to only speak with them within the context of other people, it's more beneficial. If they begin to speak it is at least a negative energy is spread to everyone in the group and not just you. People also tend to display their best aspect when speaking with several people.

4. Be neutral

Negative people find fault with other people every day. She is only able to see the mistakes or flaws, as well as deficiencies all the time. She can also be quite outspoken about this. Know that she doesn't intend to harm anyone and it's just a matter of from her character as an uninformed person. Do not take her words as personal and try to remain objective regarding what she's saying. If you can, try to show and assist her in recognizing the positive aspect of an issue. Say to her "that's the way you see it but how do you explain it to her? ..."

5. Gradually introduce optimism

Slowly bring positivity into every interaction you meet. Most often, the person's condition is due to the absence of positive influences on her. It's not your responsibility to bring her happiness or make her better overall quality of life, however, you can make small contribution at the very least where you have the chance to mix. By consistently following these guidelines, you'll slowly by little help her live positive living without her knowing.

Chapter 9: Locate A Thread Common To All And Sew It Up!

There are times when we have something we share with someone else. One of the most important aspects in building relationships is to have an affinity with another person. One way to gauge this is to look at the work environment of the person. There are typically clues that provide a glimpse of the person's past. Knickknacks, photos, memorabilia These are all things that can reveal a lot about the person. When you are getting in the middle, each friend you've met has something that is similar to you. How did you meet your most cherished friend? We met some at school, while others we were at work with in our local area or through a acquaintance...

Okay So you don't desire to have a relationship with this colleague. It's true that being colleagues is much more enjoyable than feeling miserable Isn't it? Even if it's for 8 hours every day, for 5 days of the week, it is definitely feasible. There is no requirement to spend time with them at night or on weekends. Be nice! (You never think about it, but this person could end up being your most trusted friend.)

The discovery of a common thread could create that connection two people require to be in touch. Look for photos of kids--grandkids--pets--hobbies. At some point you'll discover a commonality. Once this occurs then the door will open. Use this thread to keep the communication lines open. The power of compliments is to start the conversation in a positive way. Beginning with a positive attitude usually sets the tone for the conversation.

If we are looking at the neighbor, look for that commonality--gardens, pets, cars. Utilize these topics to start an interesting discussion with your neighbour. Discuss their garden with them. How do they keep bugs away? Which kind of fertiliser are they using? The majority of people, even elderly people, enjoy having a discuss things they enjoy. Older people are also known to share their advice. Even in the absence of any interest about the subject being interested will give you both an opportunity to smile and wave hello to one another. It can open up a channel of communication that could make you both becoming good neighbors.

It's worth the effort to find ways to be a good co-exister with others. You don't know when the person might be the one to help save your life, or be there for you when you need someone. Stranger things have occurred.

Chapter 10: Resolving Conflicts

Jeanette Charles and Jeanette Charles have a background in biologists. They were paired to collaborate on an research project. From the very beginning, Jeanette decided her colleague was unhappy and didn't possess the skills required to effectively work as members of a team in a challenging task.

In the space of two months, Jeanette was at the bottom of her plow. The problem was that not only was Charles the same socially ignorant as a piece of wood and he was also unable to share his data from his research with Jeanette. The atmosphere inside the tiny laboratory, where they would spend whole days in the same space, became uncomfortable. Jeanette discovered it was harder to sleep and more difficult, and her work started to fall behind. She bled out with pimples even though she'd never experienced pimples prior to this. Her dermatologist immediately found that her skin condition was a result of stress.

After an argument that was out and about between Jeanette and Charles, Jeanette decided to find out the truth about the matter. She questioned colleagues who were acquainted with Charles and attempted to discover more the reasons behind his behaviour. Each time he was antagonistic towards her, she was certain to note the reasons for the disagreement.

This is the question Jeanette was able to ask herself after she uncovered the root causes that led to Charles his behavior that was causing him to be negative, and was able to determine her role in the matter.

If you're facing someone who, like Charles is afflicted by the ups and downs that life brings - such as personal devastations, frustrations with ambitions, conflicts in the workplace and so on. It is possible to overtake the barriers between you without harming either person or yourself, and at simultaneously assert yourself to your advantage.

Here's how:

Set up a time to meet with the other party. If you need to, schedule the date and time. Be sure that you don't get interrupted and also show the other person that you are taking the issue seriously.

Begin the discussion by saying that you think the situation between you isn't completely clear. There's something wrong.

Watch for the reaction of the person.

Based on how the person responds - or doesn't respond to your hints Decide what kind of "difficult" person you're working with.

Be diplomatic! For instance, when Jeanette scheduled a meeting with Charles and Charles, she didn't walk directly out to declare, "Oh, I know everything about the circumstances surrounding your job change and also about your anxiety because you didn't attend an outstanding school!"

Be careful not to be rude or arrogant. Finally, something that we aren't able to say frequently enough: DO NOT try to read the OTHER person's thoughts. There's nothing more frustrating than that. What would you think of yourself when someone did this to you?

Example:

Here's how Jeanette began to get the conversation going:

"I sense there's a tension between us and it's starting to impact our work. I don't have the same experience as you do and I had hoped to gain knowledge, and improve my techniques through cooperating with you. However, that's not the case. Do you think that we're not compatible? Are it the errors I've made that bother you? Do you think it's the method I employ? I'd love to hear what you think regarding it."

Stop trying to influence other people's minds.

It is perhaps one of the primary aspects of achievement in human relationships. We appear to have the ability to create illusions about people around us, and particularly about the people we cherish. We tend to love people regardless of their shortcomings, but just because we wish that they'll eventually alter and be more similar to our ideal image of them.

We have spent years trying to convince someone to change how we want them to. Until the time comes that we realize that changing a person is beyond our capabilities and especially when the change we're trying to create is against the person's personal preferences.

The moment comes the time comes when we either begin loving the person for who she/he is, or end up not loving them at all This is the place where the risk is.

Human beings can change

This does not mean that individuals have the ability to make changes.

It is clear that every human being changes throughout the course of his or his or her life. The environment influences us to alter, as is the exercise of our individual will, and this goes on until a very advanced years.

However, it is in the first 12 years of their lives that they are the most flexible. However, even in the beginning of our lives it is a huge difficult time getting our children follow our desires.

It is a given that once someone reaches adulthood, their development is completely out of the influence of anyone else in normal conditions.

Think about the most recent time you had an unpleasant or difficult interaction with someone and you thought to yourself "If you could only be less tight!" or "If only you were a bit more accommodating ..." and "If only older people weren't so demanding ..." as well as "If you could only get my children to be more considerate ..." and so on.

Our desires are not real

Our mistake is based on the belief that other people should be able to conform to our expectations and, when they do not meet our standards then we blame them. We call them difficult, uncaring, selfish or excessively demanding, undecisive, or arrogant and so on.

The most important thing is to recognize the fact that you're dealing with an actual person and that each person has their own strengths and weaknesses. People are not the product of our imaginations It is impossible to eliminate any the aspects of their personalities that don't live up to our expectations or assign them traits we believe they should have.

It's the reason I'm always happy whenever someone says "You're dissatisfying me." For me, this implies that they aren't in touch with me as I truly is, but instead, the image of who they believe I is - or in other words they are in touch with their own self-image. Imagine how much time we are the screen for other people's projections!

The best option is to recognize the real-world situation of those who are around us, both those who are pleasing to us and those who do not. We must also realize that we have the ability to contribute to their happiness and self satisfaction in the event that they would like us to contribute.

You can influence the attitudes of people
Although you can try to make the best effort to improve the relationship between you and someone else, if you are a "difficult" person but you should not under any ever attempt to change the person's character. You won't succeed and, in all likelihood, it will not help in any way.

What you are able to change is a person's perception of you. This is the goal to concentrate all efforts.

You are more helpful to the person in this manner instead of trying to alter the person's personality and help make the person more comfortable to get along with from your perspective Of course.

In bringing the issue or conflict that's poisoning your relationship to public, you aid the other person to see better and in the same way that you've been able see yourself clearly because of your efforts.

And it is only by realizing those forces and goals of our hearts, the desires and the displeasures that cause us to do certain things, which allows us to manage our lives, assert ourselves , and find fulfillment.

You can distance yourself

When confronted with a conflicting relationship, we can become completely involved. It is difficult to maintain objectiveness. Our lives can be affected because we are absorbed by the issue. It is possible to become obsessed with the person who is difficult that is in the spotlight and the issues he/she causes.

This was what happened first to Jeaneatte our biologist. Devastated by her struggles with Charles the biologist, she found herself unrestful and couldn't perform her job properly, until she took control of herself and began to analyze the situation as if was an outsider.

But staying away from someone who has an enormous influence is more easily to say than do. The most difficult people are able to figure out how to create negative emotions - they are always able to figure out exactly what to say or do to upset us.

Implement a plan and follow it

When it comes to dealing with difficult individuals, there are only two strategies to pick from. Or, you engage in a battle of wills in hopes of winning. You are looking for ways to get satisfactory results while taking another person's preferences into consideration.

The upper hand

As we've learned in previous sections we've discussed the different kinds of "difficult" people therefore, the strategy we employ will be based on the kind of attack you're being a victim of.

In this case, if you're dealing with a negative person who is able to gradually stimulate your mind with moderate doses of pessimism and despair, you'll be less likely to be drawn into a situation of power struggle in comparison to when you're dealing with the "steamroller" kind of.

If we take a look at all the things around us we observe that the battle for survival is the frantic battle of life, in which the large fish devour the small ones, while the stronger prevail over the weak. Therefore, there is a huge possibility to view our relationships with people who are difficult as a fight, where all that matters is to win the advantage.

But, you've probably observed that in the previous sections we've not suggested that getting the upper hand is the primary goal of your education in interpreters in all relationships.

Avoid situations that result in losing or winning

The reason behind this strategy is that whenever you're in the situation of a lose-win that the person who lost will not stop until they have come up with a method of getting revenge. This could be a response as "natural" since it's very widespread.

However, if you look at it, you'll realize that while the animal kingdom relies on the balance that is created by the powerful devouring less powerful animals, nowhere does we find animals that are weak and waiting for a long time, sometimes even generations in order to reverse the balance and take justice on another creature to redress a previous affront.

This is a distinctly human characteristic that is well-known and can lead to all sorts of disasters : wars hunger, repression, unnecessary destruction, and more.

That's why our suggestions are focused on "restoring communication back to the level when it stopped" in addition to "defining your position and that of the person in question in the event of a need." Don't let anyone walk over you does not necessarily mean that you should be a slave to the person. It's about not letting someone else rule you and, in light of this affirmation of your self doing something positive about the situation.

Strategies for win-win as well as the games of life

A different approach to approaching our interactions with others is to work towards creating an environment that meets our requirements and the other person's.

There are those who we do not feel any special feelings, yet they surprise us with the kind and uninvolved acts they show for us. Every time we feel like an individual winner in our relationships with them, we're conscious or not, making a point to their favor. It could be that day when they perform something that changes the balance and this time positively and we are being overwhelmed with gratitude to them.

A narrow perspective on life can give us the perception that nature is just an enormous field of battle. However, science has proven that, more than anything nature is an investigation of balance. If a species goes extinct due to a predator's success then the predator too will go extinct due to insufficient food.

The further we advance in our understanding of the universe more and more we realize that everything is connected to the rest of the universe. By causing someone else to lose eventually puts yourself in a position to be a victim too. This is how the game of life plays out. We're all on the same boat. And should I create holes in your hull of the boat because I want that you sink then I'm going to sink as well.

What is taking place now, due to advances in communication and science, is a change in consciousness that is unimaginable in human history. We are finding that winning by losing others is not a realistic option in the slightest. The true choice is either we all win together or we both lose together. That's the only option we have. That's why it is imperative to adopt a win-win mindset that is so strong that it becomes a habit in all circumstances.

When we're working with nice pleasant, friendly, and easy-going people, it's natural. We see certain people as "disarming" and can't even imagine doing anything that could hurt them, possibly because we'd feel ashamed afterward.

However when we need to confront difficult people it becomes much more difficult, possibly due to the fact that we feel they've done us wrong in some way and we would like to punish them.

We have the option

In these kinds of situations, we can choose between building a relationship on dominance and force and dominance, a relationship that is certain to fail in the end or looking at ways to please both of the parties.

When confronted by a challenging person, you must be clear about the strategy you're planning to employ Are you planning to take on the person you are fighting to enjoy the pleasure (albeit only for a short time) of winning or retribution without thinking about the cost you'll pay for the joy later?

Are you planning to first protect yourself, and then seek ways to begin a constructive conversation?

These two choices are always open to you. The only thing that is different in this case is the approach you choose to take.

Be aware of interactions that can be negative

The most significant issue when using the win-win approach in that negative energy that defines the conversation can create more negative feelings in the person you are communicating with. This is exactly what's meant by negative interactions - the vicious circle.

Sometimes, they're impossible to avoid. We're all so frustrated and angry that any chance of improving the situation or bringing the issue to a resolution appears to be very unlikely.

If you're the victim of slander, anger or injustice, it may be difficult to keep your cool and to not respond in a similar manner.

But, if you'd like be assertive, change situations, or aid another person simultaneously you are left with no other choice. It is important to learn how to control your reactions so that you can break the cycle of negativity and create the cycle of positive interactions instead.

What you're expected to do in order to calm conflict situations and to begin communicating with people who are difficult should be to deal with the anger of their rage with patience and to their disrespect with respect and to their destructive motives with compassion.

If you believe that this is an impossible task only reserved for angels or saints and saints, then you'll undoubtedly perpetuate the cycle of mistrust and violence that you come across. However, despite the fact that the way you react might be reserved for "evolved" people but it is by no way beyond the capabilities of any human being.

The the fact that you've read this far provides enough evidence that developing these reflexes will not be a major issue for you. All you need to do is perform the exercises that are suggested later.

In the end, you must strive for positive interactions

There's a good thing In the same manner that negative is attracted to negative, positive is attracted to positive. The most difficult job is to reverse the currenttrend, and we'll look at several ways of making this happen.

We've previously stressed how important it is to avoid reacting to aggression by displaying aggression. It is important to mention it once more, as it is the basis of making any major modifications in your difficult or conflicting relationships.

We have looked at how difficult people are to bring out our worst side or dropping us to their level, such that we do exactly what we've been accusing them of doing! Don't forget, regardless of how difficult someone may appear, they are capable of reacting positively to the appropriate type of stimuli; everyone (almost) has all the required resources to be an person who is open, positive and a open-minded person.

To begin your journey, you should be the first to declare your absolute refusal to participate in any game that is destructive. When attempts to get you involved in these games end and you are able to begin working as the motor that drives the relationship towards a positive one.

Remove all your junk and trash that are weighing your down. Begin to accumulate "golden points" throughout your interactions. Set up conditions for positive interactions that will create "virtuous" circles rather than destructive ones. I am sure that your life will go through an incredible transformation to the positive.

Chapter 11: The Gossip

There are plenty of gossips in companies with poor management practices or ones that have a number of organizational challenges. If not handled properly gossips can lead to serious issues in the workplace. The negative effects of gossip can lower morale among employees and lead to the loss of productivity and inefficiency. Here are some suggestions on how to handle employees who enjoy gossip around the workplace.

Be sure to set an example that is positive

This is especially true for supervisors and managers who are looking to limit or stop gossip in the workplace. It is essential to ensure that you don't propagate gossip to prevent others from claiming that they're only doing what you say. Don't talk about your coworkers particularly your boss. Don't speculate on idle topics. Don't make a fuss about the company's policies before your coworkers. If you are a fan of doing these kinds of things, don't be shocked when those below you are doing exactly the same thing you're doing. If you set a great example, your employees will have an example to follow and emulate.

Be open to receiving concerns and issues

If your colleagues feel that you're not willing to listen to their concerns regarding issues and workplace issues In some cases, they will resort to gossip to express their opinions. If they believe they can't speak with you directly, they discuss their issues among themselves. If they feel that you're not ready to provide them with clear answers to their questions and questions, they'll get into a discussion.

Make sure your communication lines are accessible

You shouldn't just listen to the concerns and problems of subordinates and coworkers, however, you must also make sure you properly share details that your team members and subordinates should be aware of. Don't make them ask for information from anyone else. If there are problems to be addressed it is best to be open with your team members so that you can co-operate and work towards a solution. Transparency within your team will allow you to build trust and the support of your team, which will reduce gossip and speculation.

A lot of gossip starts with someone "shoots at the person who is in charge". Don't take any negative action like dissing people who bravely bring up issues to you. If you do they won't take the initiative to discuss the issue with you. Subordinates and coworkers could choose to simply complain and argue among themselves rather than bear the burden.

Find out how to tackle those who are known for spreading gossip

If rumormongers can broadcast their gossips without negative consequences, they'll believe that it is okay to do it. However should you inform a rumormonger that you are aware of the gossip that he's been telling regarding you, then the person who spreads the gossip will probably stop sharing the gossip. In fact, he may be compelled to stop his gossip once it is discovered that his gossips could harm others' opinions. If you confront someone regarding the gossips they have spread, you'll not just stop the person from spreading gossips, but you'll also stop other people from telling the stories.

Learn to deal with the issue, not those who are spreading the news.

If you do choose to take on a gossip-monger It is recommended to concentrate on the topic being discussed about and the behaviour of the other party, and not focussing on the individual. You'll appear better professional doing this. In lieu of saying"You are a scumbag for spreading gossip about me" instead, you could choose to say"I'm worried about the gossips you're spreading, and I'd like you to stop spreading them." If you respond in this manner, you will not seem like an antagonist to anyone else who might be watching your conversation.

Don't let yourself get swept up in the circumstances

One of the most effective ways to stop gossip and rumors at work is to avoid being sucked into. If someone is urging you to statement about someone who is not there it is possible to decline and change the topic in a subtle way. If you choose to do this it will stop the gossip from be allowed to continue growing and the people will have more interesting things to discuss.

Find out the truth about the validity of gossips by asking questions

There are occasions where you are getting caught up in gossip, and you are unable to just shift the conversation to something else. If find yourself in this situation then you should confirm the facts they're talking about. Be sure to ask questions about the exact date, time, and other details. It is likely that people don't realize that they are only aware of some basic facts about the topic which is being debated. If you request specifics, you're really forcing the issue with a subdued manner, because anyone who is unable to provide specific details basically admits to the falsity of the information being circulated. If gossipmakers aren't able to give you specific information then you can say back"I believe all the information is very vague. Are you sure that it's real?" By saying this you are clear in telling gossips that there are doubts about what they're telling you.

Try to come up with solutions

There are many gossips that occur when employees or employees are worried about a particular subject. When you witness people beginning to discuss or complain and gossip, remember the old saying"It is more beneficial to light a single candle rather than beg the dark." Instead of contributing to the complaining and rants, you can help others to think about solutions. Don't expect to always have solutions that management would readily accept. However, focussing on solutions can stop individuals from spreading gossip.

Avoid being self-righteous

If you're using any of the methods mentioned above, it is important be careful not to do it in a self-righteous fashion. Do not boast about the efforts you have made to stop gossips. It is best to be careful not to become egocentric and begin telling your coworkers that gossiping is not good. If you are self-righteous, you'll end up alienating your coworkers. It is best to remain gentle when dealing with gossip so that you do not create problems you have to resolve.

Chapter 12: Strategies For Non-Confrontational Behavior To Handling Difficult People At Work

There are people who have difficulty everywhere, including at work. While their presence cause work to be more stressful, they're in a position to hinder your professional growth. The ability to deal with difficult people is contingent on three aspects:

* Your self-esteem level
* Your self-confidence.
* Your professional grit

It is possible to ask "why is it necessary to deal with these issues?" Can you not simply ignore them and carry on in your job? The thing about people who are difficult is that when problems are not addressed they can get worse. In the absence of resolution, it will not result in the tension disappearing. It will instead simmer beneath the surface, creating negative feelings. It's not something you'd like to endure over the long term but not when it has a negative impact on your job and the satisfaction you get from your work.

If someone behaves in a manner that is not professional You may be shocked and wounded. If you leave the issue unresolved for a long time could lead to you snapping in the end. If you address the issue as quickly as you can, you'll be competent to deal with it in an objective and calm manner. Instead of figuring out solutions to the employee who is difficult, many individuals just settle for complaining. The problem with this is that you'll gain the reputation of being a complainer. Management will see you as an individual who's incapable of solving your own issues.

In the worst case scenario the inability of you to manage difficult colleagues can cause others to view you as an unlikable person too. This can be a stickiness that is difficult to remove and can result in a negative impact on not just your image , but your career too. In addition, if the issue persists in a state of confusion and is received with only endless complaints, your boss may decide that you're an employee who is high maintenance and that you should be replaced by someone more professional and is able to work with colleagues. This isn't a good thing especially in the current employment market where there's many skilled workers being let go.

What should you do? Do you want to leave a bottle of powdered feet for someone who has smelly feet? Do you put an ant in the office drawer? Do you confront your coworker with the intention of encouraging coworkers to attack him? The methods you are using appear to be a bit juvenile and could result in your being fired. Are you dreading working just to avoid a certain person? Do you feel you have to do something but aren't sure how to confront your troublesome coworker? If yes then it might be a good idea to begin with an approach that is non-confrontational.

Examine yourself.

Sometimes, the strength you require isn't necessarily to confront your coworker and admit that you're not right. The first step is determine if you're the only person who's affected by your coworker's difficult attitude. If your colleagues can see the same person as a problematic individual, then it's not your blame. Conduct an honest evaluation of yourself. Think about: Is the issue partially caused by me? Do I have anything could I do help the situation?

Take care to protect yourself.

Even if you're eager to be a victim, you should take a step back. Establish boundaries for yourself. Be mindful of your words and whom you speak it to. Although the desire to backstab to gain sympathy appear to be irresistible at times but you could be prone to saying things you regret later. If you have to discuss the problem with someone, make sure to confide in people who are reliable and not just anyone willing to listen. If you can it is best to avoid speaking about the issue to people who have no idea about the issue and are not involved in the matter. Avoid involving any person who is not capable of finding solutions to the issue. Although you may think inviting your peers to form an internal support system is an excellent idea, keep in mind that the most important thing you should do is to maintain the respect of your colleagues.

Know your reaction.

The way you react to the behavior of the person who is difficult will give you an idea of the motive behind his behavior is. Have they succeeded in manipulating with you? Do you give him precisely what he wants?

Be aware of your emotions. Consider whether the actions of your coworker cause you to feel inferior or undervalued. Do you have anger that you later regret? Do you ever say "yes" even though what you ought to be saying should be "no"? Do you feel your voice is being muffled and is it preventing the possibility of sharing creative ideas during business meetings?

After an honest assessment make sure you decide if your reaction is appropriate to the circumstance or if you're overreacting.

Discover the motive.

What is the reason they do this? To resolve your issue with a coworker who is difficult You must first figure the motives behind his behavior. Find out if there's some reason behind this behavior. Find out the reason. People who have difficulty with coworkers usually fall into two groups. They include those who are attracted by attention, and those who are averse to attention.

The Know-it-all

They tend to appear superior and often are humorous. They are able to make themselves feel better in the process of making you appear unqualified. They address you with a the manner of a snarky tone and exhibit aggressive behavior.

The Bully

These individuals are aggressive, and, sometimes, even hostile. They are loud and powerful They can even harass you.

The Complainer

People who complain loudly about their troubles. They tend to drain your energy and waste a good portion of your time focusing on their complains. Sometimes, they ask them to solve their problems.

The Silent Type Silent Type

This includes coworkers that are difficult to converse with. They are difficult to talk to. getting their attention.

The Yes Person

They tend to be adamant about every single thing. They appear to be in agreement with almost everything. They appear to be good at first, but then you realize they are not able to fulfill their promises.

The Negativist

Pessimists complain about every issue. They tend to sabotage the overall atmosphere of work as their negative feelings often are infectious.

The Worker Who Is Undecided

They are not capable of making their own choices. They are always waiting for your intervention. Their dependence can become toxic as time passes.

It is important to note that all the personalities listed above have selfish behaviours. They are all trying to achieve what they want, and usually at your cost. How do you deal with these people?

Pay attention and you'll see that the four categories of people listed exhibit attention-delaying behaviors. They often get the encouragement, support and motivation.

The first three people on this list display an interest-seeking behavior. This issue can be solved without provoking them by refusing to reward the behavior of these people. If you continue to feed them with attention in turn, you're inducing the difficult behavior. Here's how to ensure harmony and keep peace

Make the most of your time in the same room.

Avoid direct communication with the person.

Make it more challenging for the attackers to get in touch with you.

If an email sent by this person is not important or has absolutely nothing to have to do with work, either you dismiss the message or assign the email to someone else.

This doesn't look like a lot of courage, is it? Perhaps. However, it avoids unnecessary conflicts and helps you keep the courtesy of a civilized society. What happens if these nifty methods don't be effective? Learn what you can do in the next chapters.

Chapter 13: Tips To Manage The Dominant, Pushy Persona Of Bully By Being Assertive

Dealing with a bully or any other person who is dominant and abusive can be overwhelming, particularly when the person who is being bullied is a coworker or an individual from your family or a friend. There are some tips to help you become more assertive when taking a stand. It is essential to know how to assert yourself in order to eliminate the bullies you deal with every day.

Examine the situation and avoid Self-blaming

If you feel like you're a victim to bullying, or possess an excessively assertive personality, it's crucial to recognize that it isn't the fault of anyone else or was even initiated by you, rather it's an issue that's ascribed to the person who is bullying you. Being free of responsibility when confronting an aggressive person can allow you find some relief as you gain confidence in yourself.

Consider the reason you think that you are being bullied, and what you can do to keep the bully out of your workplace or at home. This will help you distance yourself from the bully physically as well as physically. By turning away from the bully, and ignoring any anger or self-deflection that the bully may switch to someone who is thought of as "weaker" or is a better to target.

Make sure you are kind to yourself

Make use of kindness in getting rid of a bully when you're not a fan of confrontation. Even though avoiding confrontation and being kind to the bully in all circumstances isn't always helpful but it can help to feel at tranquility in the midst of the conflict. When you remove yourself from the negative feelings that the bully often evokes, it can help you be less anxious. Nod, smile and accept and then get away from someone who is overly insecure, aggressive or behaves as an aggressive bully.

Then, you can present yourself as an assertive

Improve how you stand by being up straight and making use of the letter "I" when you speak and making direct eye contact to bullies or people with confident personality. This can assist you in becoming more confident in yourself. If you appear confident and confident, you'll be capable of displaying confidence that is usually disregarded by potential bullies as well as those who seem to be domineering.

Also, you can improve your confidence and assertiveness by practicing your responses and conversations with family members and acquaintances. Do not show any weaknesses in your facial expressions or emotions even when angered by rude individuals. By placing fingers on the hips when standing up straight is a way to demonstrate your power. It also assists in stopping bullies from coming up to you only to lift or to gain satisfaction from making an issue within you at any moment.

Keep calm

If you're confronted by bullies or someone who is prone to dominating conversations and assertive, be as calm as you can to not show that you're intimidated. Avoiding showing emotion could signal to the bully that you're as confident. Instead, make an empathetic "poker face" without emotion if you are being scolded or yelled at. In extreme cases, criticized. Be sure to identify someone who is excessively aggressive and bully, especially if you're in a work environment in a group.

People who are dominant and bullies are not gone as we graduate from elementary school. They are everywhere around us in our families or in our workplace. When you become confident and assertive the bully will no longer consider you a simple victim. They'll be more likely to let you go. Make use of these strategies to restore the confidence you had over a dominant or bully personality.

Chapter 14: Do Not Take It Personally

A major reason difficult people cause many problems is that they tend to be a victim of their behavior. If you believe you are a difficult person, is an intention to smack you in the face and you interpret their behavior as a sign people don't like you, then you'll be a long time in your life feeling very wounded. The best way to deal with people who are difficult is to not take their actions as a personal attack.

You must realize that some people are acting out because of reasons that are entirely unrelated to you. It could be one of the reasons I mentioned in the previous paragraphs. It could be a totally different reason that nobody else has ever heard of. It's likely not solely due to your actions. In rare instances is the difficult behavior of someone else targeted at you.

If your mind stops taking situations personally, you will stop worrying about the actions of other people. It is possible to begin your process of eliminating or balancing others' challenging behavior. There are a variety of things you can try instead of being angry or frustrated by issues with others. What are some things you can do instead of engaging in a personal attack? Try a more positive approach towards difficult people rather than a hurtful and personal approach to change difficult encounters into positive ones.

Consider Difficult People as a challenge

Are you interested in knowing the factors that set successful entrepreneurs and salespeople apart from other people? It's all in the mental attitude. The most successful people are more likely to look at difficult situations and people as enjoyable problems. They accept the difficult and strive to "win" when they encounter difficult people. They do not take their problems personal or surrender in despair.

It is essential to start looking at difficult people in this manner you would view them. Consider how this could be a an opportunity to transform someone's perspective. Try to improve the situation instead of fighting it or causing the situation.

Empathize

Empathy can make life much simpler for all. When you are empathetic you begin to comprehend the reasons why people make the choices you do. You become gentler and understanding. You are able to avoid a number of confusions. It is easier to forgive others for their mistakes once you know what they felt while they did something.

Take a moment to consider things from the perspective of someone else before you make any conclusions. Rethinking your viewpoint is the first step to developing compassion. Think about their current life situations and their personality. Take into consideration that you might be the one to trigger them into having some reaction. Be aware of how prepared they might be to deal with situations effectively. If you attempt to see things from the perspective of someone else you could be able to discern the motivation behind someone's taking certain actions.

For instance those who have experienced an abusive childhood is likely not have the most effective strategies for dealing with relationship issues. If you and your partner disagree, he will completely shut down and blocks you. If you don't want to take the situation personal and thinking that he might just hate you, think about the difficulties it poses for him to manage the stress of a relationship. Give him a second chance and be honest with him about your desires. "I am aware that you are not a fan of fighting. However, I am irritated when you stop fighting. Would you be able to talk with me, instead of closing me out?" is something that you could ask the person.

Look for the Cause of the Difficulty

It is best for you to take a proactive approach and take life in a positive approach. When someone isn't being helpful or difficult, simply drowning in your rage is ineffective. Instead, it's more successful trying to solve the issue. Finding out why someone is difficult will help you discover ways to improve the behavior.

Start by encouraging the openness of dialogue. Have you ever thought of asking someone who is difficult what is bothering them? Do it, and you may be amazed at how they will relax. People aren't familiar with having people take care of them. If you show that you be caring, people are likely to become more friendly towards you and even work with you. They will see that you're not as bad after all.

Find an equilibrium

Know that it's not your fault.

One of the most important aspects of not being a victim of things is understanding that the majority of what people do isn't your responsibility. Individuals have their own challenges. They are most of the time focused on their own problems, which means that they don't understand how their actions affect other people. Although this isn't a reason for being rude, it does clear the way for you to be blameless when others are irritable around you.

Certain people are selfish. They focus on their own desires that they don't consider your own personal sanctity and happiness. Don't blame yourself for being weak. Don't blame them for being a disaster to you. You need to be more assertive later on, yet don't blame yourself for being trusting and kind.

Don't Make People a Definition

It is simple to judge people on the basis of their actions. We are taught to place more importance on actions than words, and with good reason. the actions of others usually speak louder over their own words. If someone displays an unsettling behavior it is best to keep your judgment until the future. The definition of a person is not always based through their behavior.

It's normal to believe, "He is such an asshole" or "She is such a jerk" after seeing unflattering behaviour in some one. However, it is not advisable to think of these things right away. It is best to give an individual an opportunity to reconsider before you decide to label them as a threat to your reputation and ban them from your life for good. There is a chance to find a wonderful colleague or the perfect friend in someone and don't just write them off on the basis of a single review. Do you want to have someone forever be negative about your character because you had an unlucky day and behaved in a way that was terribly wrong?

Be aware of someone's behaviour throughout time before you reach an assessment. Don't make your assessments on someone's character based on an incident. Instead, take a look at their overall attitude and behavior over a variety of events.

Avoid Drama

There are a variety of alternatives when you meet someone who is difficult. The first option is to let them be a victim. Another alternative is to explode things to start a fight, and lots of drama. Drama is stressful and will cause friction between you and your friends. It is best to avoid drama.

It is generally recommended to be more professional than your peers in your conduct. This way, you'll appear trustworthy and mature, and will not be held accountable for any incident that occurred during a tough conversation with someone else. Be a calm and an objective observer. Avoid dramatic situations if you wish to avoid problems in the future.

You stand a possibility of negotiating with someone if you conduct yourself in a manner that is not dramatic. If you act in a way that is dramatic it is likely that you will cause a lot of friction and ruin any chances of settling issues.

Don't let it affect you.

Don't let the actions of others alter the person you are. If someone is difficult, it's human nature to seek to change. You become apathetic You become angry, you're ready to explode at others. Your mood and attitude will change as a result of conflict.

However, be aware that the conduct of other people actually has little impact on your life. People who annoy you with their rudeness , or insincerity aren't really crucial in the long run. Think about this:

Will the behavior of this person be relevant to me in the next year? If not then don't allow this person to affect your life in such a way. Do not make changes in the direction of them or for them. Do not let his / his or her petty snark have lasting consequences for your life.

Make them like rubber and then create glue. Their words should bounce off your.

Chapter 15: What To Do To Deal With Difficult People In Public

This is in stark contrast to the those you interact with at home, you meet lots of characters and personalities in public , but only for an insignificant amount of time. There is no genuine connection that are established between them. The reason it is a challenging to think about is that these times are brief, it is due to the fact that you're exposed many different factors.

Try not to be distracted and remain cool.

Since you're in contact with them for a brief duration, it's recommended to avoid them whenever you are able to. Giving a little patience to the people you meet in public can help you avoid conflicts and creating the scene.

What the possibility of confronting everyone who made you angry in the public? It would be an uncontrollable riot. Consider it this way also, what advantage do you gain when you confront someone? If the cost is greater than the reward then it is best to wait and let the issue go. With the numerous similar decisions you make every day, the chances are that at the close of the week you'll be unable to remember the person who put onto your new pair of shoes while on the subway on Monday, or the person who took your taxi on Tuesday.

These are situations that will not have any impact in five years' time So don't let a few moments consume or affect your day to day activities, as more important events will occur.

Don't be a jerk

When you see how unimportant these moments are, it'll be less difficult for you to make a noise about it. It is possible to claim that the premise of the situation is greater than the actual situation. The most straightforward solution is to decide which fights to take on.

Situations like this don't need to be exaggerated. Keep in mind that there are more worthy causes in your life, and more significant people therefore, you should concentrate your efforts on those things and people that are important to you.

Let them know your intentions clearly
If you must communicate your need with a calm and respectful manner regardless of how angry or annoyed you feel. The public is more inclined listen to and respond to those with a calm disposition and are not swept off by emotions.

The issue could be that they did not realize that they're irritating you. When you make a point of pointing it the matter your concerns to them, then the problem can be resolved easily. Keep in mind that, like you they also must endure the pressure hundreds of others each day.

Be the judge - get away if you can.

If circumstances permit it, you should make the move to make sure you're not impacted by the circumstances. It's not as difficult as transferring seats at the cinema or shutting out the world by listening to music on your headphones. Don't let your environment affect you.

Decide to be the more powerful person and get to your ideal spot. The world is exactly as you want you to see it, and so keep your eyes on the positives, instead of dwelling on things that frustrate you.

How to approach difficult people

After you've seen the various kinds of people who are difficult, and their particular characteristics We can now consider how to deal with the people who are difficult. When we say approach, we are referring to how to react to someone who is difficult, and how to behave with them. Here are some key tips on how to handle this:

1. Take a break for a minute

The most difficult people tend to be provocative when you're having conversations with them. This is why you must find ways to calm your nerves in the event of this. What can you do to achieve this? It's as simple as breathing deeply and taking a time to relax your mind and gather your thoughts prior to responding to any question they might have asked. This will help you calm your nerves and clear your mind before you respond swiftly and say something that you later regret.

This method can also delay the flow in an argument. For instance, if an angry person attacks you, he/she typically tries to provoke your to confront them. When you respond and they escalate the fight until you are acting as the person they are. But, if you stop frequently in your thinking, it helps dissipate the argument and they stop being abusive since the abuse isn't getting to you.

2. Be cool and stay cool

Another method of dealing with the person who is difficult is to keep your cool. Like we discussed in the last chapter, the most difficult people may come on very strongly. They might use insults against you (stupid and idiot) or make you appear dumb, and may even make fun of you. It can be difficult to take in. In order to avoid falling to their level it is important to keep your cool and fight your cool.

If you are doing this, the person you are yelling at will notice how absurd they sound in yelling, and think about the actions of that person. This way, you totally dispel their motives. Try this next time someone who is difficult appears to you.

3. Pick your battles carefully

If you are ever in a situation in which you could be in a heated dispute with someone who is difficult it is important to ask yourself if what you're discussing is something worthy of fighting for. You might be surprised to realize that you typically fight over the same thing.

It is best to avoid debates over issues that don't add any value. You should only engage in debates on issues that matter in your daily life. You might argue with your boss regarding the number of hours you've been working. But when it comes to fighting over who has the better phone, you can let the battle be over.

4. Be truthful

The most difficult people, like the complainer can easily spark arguments. So, it is important to be extremely cautious not to say anything incorrect when speaking with someone who is difficult. If you know the someone's trigger subjects, stay clear of engaging in conversation about these issues. One example is when politics are the trigger for someone you know. If this is the case, when you're around the person, it is best to avoid the subject and focus on other subjects.

There are times when you will encounter an adversarial person who constantly comes up with a reason to debate. In this case, keep your conversations to facts. It can be challenging to convince someone of your viewpoint however, you shouldn't try to justify your position in an attempt to convince the person. This method has been proven to be highly efficient when dealing with an elusive to understand person.

5. Speak up in support of your rights and requirements

The difficult people, like the people who know everything would prefer everything to follow their own way and are not convinced that they can learn anything. If you are dealing with this kind of person, you need to speak more clearly. Be confident and clear.

When you encounter a less than knowledgeable person, challenge their ignorant ideas by staying calm and playing cool. Then make corrections to their statements. One good example is using words such as. "I am aware of your frustrations over the slow pace that this endeavor is taking. If you were me, I'd be just as frustrated. Unfortunately, this type of project usually takes a while to finish."

6. Reduce interactions

People with difficulties are everywhere, and you'll be faced with one or another. This might not be an easy task but you can reduce the burden of these situations by doing everything possible, staying clear of, or reducing interactions between individuals. If you are required to communicate with someone who is difficult make sure to be as courteous and positive as you can.

It is possible to do this by making your conversations brief whenever you encounter this type of person. If this doesn't work then you may try other strategies like letting yourself go for two minutes conversation , or inviting a third party that can make your conversation more enjoyable.

Tips for Dealing with difficult people

Here are a few of personal suggestions you could employ when communicating with people who are difficult to talk to.

Look for positive relationships. This can help you balance your life, balancing out your negative experiences with those who are difficult.

When you're dealing with someone who is difficult there will always be unpleasant moments. The best way to handle these situations is to inject humor into these moments.

You should be cautious that you do not blame another person as the difference in your opinions and communications results from the different personalities of you. The blame game will only create a bitterness.

Keep in mind the fact that no one you speak with should be near to you. To be able to get along with other people particularly difficult people, you just need to be respectful.

Chapter 16: Enter Into Conversation

Next step engaging in dialogue. At this point, you must be able to empathize with the angered person's emotions and concerns, taken note of their needs and needs (or demands) and asked them clarifying questions and perhaps even identified common areas that are in mutual agreement. Because of your efforts, person may have settled down, and the anger may have been replaced by anger, annoyance or anger.

They ought to be capable of thinking more rationally and be able to calm enough to take in your thoughts. Now is the moment to engage in an exchange of ideas and to begin creating a mutually acceptable solution. To make this process successful, there are additional guidelines that you must adhere to.

Make it clear that you care about the issue and you really are determined to find a solution.

Always give the other person all your focus - don't get distracted.

Make use of "I" phrases when you express your viewpoint.

Be focused on the relevant facts rather than your opinion.

Find areas where there is areas of agreement.

Give them a small win.

Keep your focus on the present. An angry person is likely to refer to the past and attempt to entice you. Focus on the present issue and tell the opponent to both concentrate on the present source of the conflict and then address each issue one at a time.

Do not insist on the proof that you're right and they're wrong, as it could cause further resentment. more. Be calm and discuss your viewpoint or cite facts. It should be easy for your audience to alter their opinions without losing your face.

If keeping your focus isn't working, redirect the conversation to a different but less volatile topic. Try to find the same ground before re-entering into the issue.

Return the conversation to its original focus if you've gotten off-track.

Tips: Don't say to the person that they should calm down', as this is likely to cause more anger. Be aware that someone who is angry isn't thinking about things rationally.

What is the reason for the anger?

It is crucial to identify the root of the issue rather than simply tackling the symptoms, or else the issue could recur in the future.

Utilize empathy listen: "Tell me more" "Help me to understand". Questions that are open ended work great for helping you figure out the root of what's bothering him or her.

Most of the time it is the case that anger shields another emotion, like:

Guilt

Hurt

Loss

Anxiety

Sadness

The loneliness

Fear

The 'Counseling Center', California State University Bakersfield, says that the root of anger is due to "perceived lack of control over the factors that affect significant values." These values could be linked to love, pride and money, as well as justice, etc.

For instance, an employee of a sales team is driving across town to set up the appointment of a prospective client and is disappointed to discover that the prospect isn't available and didn't call to cancel the appointment. The emotion that is underlying could have been "hurt" (this person showed disrespect for my precious time). Another example could be one of someone who utilizes anger to help himself or herself feel better.

Certain people are extremely judgmental They blame other people for the problems they encounter and not taking accountability, and then becoming frustrated in the process. Their thought process is dominated by "should's" and "ought's" and 'musts'.

What can make one person mad could be water on the back of a duck for someone else. It's all about what they think about the situation that is influenced by their previous experiences, the triggers pulled, and the negative emotional connections, etc.

The Event that is Threatening ----> What is Interpreted

If you are able to identify the root cause behind the anger, this will allow you create an emotional distance from the anger and help you better manage it.

The Benefits of Apologizing

If the anger of the other party is justifiable and you or your company - are the reason for their anger and you are responsible and need to apologize. It is important to note that I stated 'probably' to apologize as in a professional setting, you must be aware of whether an apology may be a cause of litigation over liability.

The benefit of a properly scheduled and sincere apology, is the fact that it generally can be calming and can be an effective way to rebuild the relationship.

What's the one thing you should never do? Refuse to blame and defend your actions. It will only cause the person to become more angry. What should you do? Find out what they believe that you could do to resolve the problem.

Verbal Abuse

Don't be a victim of verbal abuse; instead, what you must do is end and delay the your conversation.

If the other person becomes violent or aggressive to harm you, immediately issue an unspoken reminder that you are not going to tolerate any such conduct and that you will end the conversation should they continue. Tell them that you'll be willing to continue the discussion after they've settled down.

If the abuse doesn't cease, repeat your statement that you won't tolerate this words, and end the conversation.

Chapter 17: Rebuilding An Adaptable Mindset

To successfully deal with challenging individuals, you must build a strong mental attitude. Resilience is the capacity to deal with everyday stress with a calm and steady attitude. People who are resilient aren't often irritated by the behavior of others and, as a result, are more likely to succeed. They can overcome any obstacle they encounter because of other people being difficult.

Edit your script

Sometimes, we respond in similarly to situations that we believe as difficult, without taking the particular circumstances into account. We do the same thing each time. For example, some people react to someone who is shouting by shouting back. This behavior is deeply ingrained in them and they have no other method of handling this situation. It is important to change our attitude when faced with difficulties. Our attitudes could be causing a situation to escalate that is deteriorating from bad to even more dire. Try to figure out what this person is trying to get with their actual motives are. Are they trying to provoke an immediate response from us? Could they be intent on obstructing us and making us feel down? Are they having difficulties in their lives? If we can understand someone and their struggles, we are in the ideal position to assist the person in a manner that is beneficial not only to us , but also them.

Be tough and resilient

The people who have a high level of stress have developed an understanding of what's important in their lives in addition to what's non-essential. They invest their time and energy doing only those things that can improve their lives. The other shows they watch are ignored. They lack the ability to handle someone who is difficult or negative. They realize that tough circumstances and people with difficult personalities are part of life and you'll come across them in your daily life, however they don't dwell on these issues. They deal with them as quickly as they can, in order to lessen the effect of these kinds of individuals on their daily lives. When you don't have any control over an event and you're able to let it go however, when you have the ability to alter the outcome of another circumstance, regardless of the difficulty that the people you're having to deal with might be.

Consider a situation from the perspective of other people

For you to remain resilient, need be able to see things from a different angle. You must be able to relate to others and be able to comprehend the reasons they're coming from. The majority of people don't choose to be difficult. They may not even consider themselves as being difficult. Their perspective on an issue could be completely different than your own. For example, people from different backgrounds might have an entirely different view regarding the issue. Understanding involves placing yourself in another person's in their shoes. It is important to behave in the way you would expect people to treat you.

Communication

A simple word spoken when spoken at the right time could stop a catastrophe from just about to happen. When dealing with people who can be difficult You must always try to effectively communicate. Communication can be done in two ways that are nonverbal and verbal. The verbal method is the most obvious however, a large portion of communication is done through nonverbal methods too. It is important to know how to recognize nonverbal signals. Certain people won't say anything to you however they'll be a nuisance. This happens in the workplace , where colleagues will ignore you and not communicate, even though you're supposed to work with each other. Also, you must learn how to communicate by non-verbal methods. Nonverbal signals can include eye movements, posture expressions, facial expressions and the use of hands. Pay attention to both nonverbal and verbal cues to receive the full reaction. Common barriers to effective communication are the assumption that the message has been accepted and understood, the making use of the inappropriate medium, the absence of emotion in delivering the message, communicating through intimidation, and the use of the incorrect communication method

Accept other people as they are

If you want determined to remain resilient, then you need to be able to accept others and understand them as they are and not expect that they will change. When you accept others, you can recognize the strengths as well as weaknesses as well as what you can do to best respond to them. Accepting someone is about having a an accurate expectations of their conduct. If you've had prior knowledge that you're dealing with an uneasy person You should be prepared for that and be prepared for it.

Being able to adapt to changes

The ability to adapt to changes is among the traits that distinguish resilient individuals. In every aspect of life changes are happening in a rapid pace and those, particularly executives who aren't able or unwilling to adjust to this change, end up struggling to deal with various types of people. The change in the world brings new possibilities, better methods of completing tasks and a greater efficiency at the workplace.

Anxiety levels are low.

To be resilient throughout life and at work it is necessary to are not anxious at all. The human nature desires us to stay where we are familiar with. We're most comfortable with the things we've done for a long time since it provides the feeling of security. If we keep doing these activities and do not change, we could become a victim of our rapid-paced life. Anxiety is the most common reason why people aren't able to from taking on a new idea. The main reason for anxiety is negative emotions, negative past events, or perhaps anxiety about the unknown.

Chapter 18: Interacting With People Who Are Difficult To Talk To

The most beneficial thing you can do in life is eliminate the bad persons from the life of yours. Make sure you surround yourself with positive people, etc. However, it's often not easy. People who are difficult come people from all walks of life. They could be acquaintances that are easy to leave close friends, somewhat uncomfortable because you are in with them the same group of acquaintances and a partner, which is an even more painful separation and the most painful and challenging of all is family. Since there are a lot of difficult people in the world, and you must know how to handle them, here are few tips to help you manage difficult individuals.

Consider if it's worth the cost

If the person who is difficult to deal with does not cause any major problems, consider whether it's worth the effort to solve your problems. The troublesome person might be with a person who is rude and is muttering about you to friends or with a partner who continuously undermines your choices or a boss inflicting a negative impact on you. When confronting someone who is difficult you must determine if it's worth trying to resolve the problem with the person. First, you must acknowledge a few things prior to making your decision.

The friendship or relationship could end or it may be able to move toward a more positive healthy, more positive relationship. Determine if it's worthwhile to talk about the issue.

It is important to determine whether the situation is so serious that it has a negative impact on your daily routine.

There aren't any issues that need to be discussed Some issues are small enough to be resolved with time, so you'll need to determine if the issue is worth the effort.

It is important to think about what your relationships are with that individual. In some cases, you'll need to accept the behavior such as when it's your manager at work in the event that it is not necessary to settle the issue, or should you be required to keep working.

Think about another aspect; is it a contest that you can beat? If no amount of argument, debate or convincing can alter their mind the best thing to do is to not keep trying.

If you've decided that the issue has to be addressed, you need arming yourself. Take all the relevant information and the details of the problem, and the solutions that are possible. It is important to be prepared be prepared for any reactions you might get from the other party.

Be aware that you're not doing this to overcome them, but rather to solve any issue you're having to resolve with them. Even if you do not confront them, there is a chance that they'll start to strike at you. Be prepared. Be aware of your emotions.

Make sure you use clear and assertive language

Most of the time, these people will make use of the words you say and use them for your own advantage, and that's why you should be careful when you speak to them, use. Make use of "I" phrases to express your emotions rather than accusing them of doing something that they might or may not have done. Examples:

"I know you were upset that I didn't get to eat the dinner you had with your family and I'm sorry I was unable to make it. I was unfortunate to have an unexpected emergency at work. I'll be able to be back the next time."

Do not say: "You are being unreasonable to believe that I will be able to make it on time for dinner, particularly when you consider that I phoned me to tell you that I will not be able finish work in time to eat dinner."

Make sure the explanations are simple

Don't go into details or justify your action. Most times, the person who is difficult won't be able understand your viewpoint and will draw their own conclusions irrespective of what you declare. The more you speak, the greater the chance of conflict. If you do speak to them,

Do not be defensive It's tempting to try to justify, and defend yourself constantly which can result in many arguments, and possibly the emergence of more issues that could create conflict instead of resolving the issues. The attempt to prove you're correct will result in wasting time and energy.

Keep calm

The most effective method of losing your grip on the situation becoming emotional. Engaging in a fight and engaging in a shouting match can only make the situation worse. When you shout at one another, the thing you need to realize that nobody is listening to the words of another is shouting at.

A key to settle any issue is to ensure you are able to have a peaceful and civil discussion. The most effective way to accomplish this is to calm the person you are talking to for them to listen.

An individual in a state of emotional state cannot listen to logic. If someone is stressed or angry what they say will be unproductive. Be calm and remain calm and focused by taking an invigorating breath.

If someone is crying, let them to calm down before approaching them to resolve the problem. You may have observed from experiences that telling someone to stop crying won't prevent them from crying.

The best method to get them to hear is sounding sensible with a calm voice, as well as not let them disturb you. If you practice this, they'll gradually recognize that they are the ones that are being a maniac and look bad. They'll settle down once they realize that you will not be infuriated.

Chat with a acquaintance or coworker

If you're having an issue with someone , and cannot resolve the issue them towards the best solution, talk to a person you know who could act as mediator. Someone you be confident in. If the issue is with your mother, perhaps your dad can get her to reach an agreement.

Perhaps it's the other student creating the problem and you can seek out an acquaintance or friend to help you resolve the issue and resolve the issue.

If you're experiencing issues with your partner, that you aren't able to resolve by yourself take your partner to a relationship counsellor.

Be careful with your interactions

If you're unable to resolve the issue, regardless of the methods you've tried, the individual isn't only difficult, but in fact, impossible. If that is the case, it is best to minimize your interactions with that person. Make your interactions brief, focused and extricate yourself from the presence the person as quickly as is possible.

Be as cool as you can throughout the conversation. Do not get involved and then collect your emotions later. overcome the impact because you know the fact that no action will alter the behaviour of the person.

Chapter 19: The Power Of Words

When Dealing With A Difficul Person

Knowing the correct word to use at the appropriate moment is a benefit over any kind of circumstance. If you are dealing with a difficult individual, the choice of words you choose to use will be a major factor. It's about fighting evil with good.

Words can do a lot. Words are extremely powerful. Words can create an enormous problem, but simultaneously, help you solve or avoid bigger issues.

The wise are recognized by the words he speaks. The fool is also known by his words. The thing you need to be aware of is that spoken words can be like a screen that reveals the condition of the heart.

The wise are identified by his carefully selected words during times of arousal While a fool is identified through the many sloppy selected phrases. One bizarre being who once stood on the earth's surface declared "out out of the abundant heart, it speaks".

Words are powerful and can be channeled to create any reason. The Bible declares that life and death are the hands that is the mouth. Your words could either make or break you.

However, connecting how words can be used to methods for dealing with a challenging person is a must. As I mentioned in chapter one , I described what I learned about my roommate, following my findings about how he responds to jokes I needed to control my laughter and be careful with my words whenever I tried to talk or joke with him. As I mentioned, it was a great solution to a number of issues.

The words you choose to use in any relationship is a significant thing to do with not talking of having to deal with someone who is difficult. If you have to maintain an amiable, smooth and enjoyable relationship with anyone, your tone of your communication and the selection of words play crucial role to play. If you have to show an immense amount of care when selecting words to address everyday people, is that any do you make yourself appear to be a more difficult person?

"A calm answer dispels anger, but a sour tone stirs up anger" These are words of wisdom from an ancient and popular king.

If you study the meaning of this phrase it will be clear that it was a reference to "stir out anger" and "not cause for anger". This clearly means that the person has to deal with an angry person and not a calm person. The answer or words need to be soft or carefully chosen to deflect or soothe the anger. If you have to gain a heart or get through a tough situation, your responses must be soothing and the anger must be avoided.

Words can be extremely effective. How you use them will determine what result you'll receive.

What are OTHER Facts Concerning Words?

The whole universe was created and placed in the world by the words of God. God brought the universe to being.

As powerful and powerful as the sun itself the sun is also a result of words coming from the mouth of God.

Words can be powerful and can be used to build or demolish.

A relationship lasting 30 - or even 50-years could be destroyed in a matter of moments if the wrong words are employed.

If not for the incorrect use of words, many of the issues that humanity is facing could not have been uncovered in the first place.

Also , if words could be correctly aligned, a lot of our issues could be a thing of the past.

Words are extremely fragile. They're just similar to eggs. If they are dropped off the tongue in a hurry and are not fixable.

Words are similar to the spit you release from your mouth. If you spill a potentially dangerous word, there's no way to take it in the future.

Silence isn't just the absence of words, but rather the power to control words or even tame them.

Silence is the most effective solution to fools, but the right usage of words can turn the fool into a wise person.

Words can be a source of inspiration or break you.

Words can be compared to seeds. If you plant the correct ones, you'll get positive results. If you plant the wrong ones, you'll see negative outcomes.

The words that come out of the mouth of wise men are like a swords. They can penetrate to the deepest parts of the body, touching the heart , and heal the soul.

If you require confessions or any other kind of confession from any mind the strength spoken words decide whether you'll get it or not. Words can reveal the secrets that lie within our hearts and expose them in a clear manner.

Your word will decide the difference between someone difficult to alter their attitude toward the other or against.

Words are the bloodline that drives communication.

Your tone can be a big factor when speaking words.

And last but not least, you should be able be able to control the force of words. You need to understand what words to use and how to use to any kind of the situation.

How can you harness the power of words when dealing with difficult people?

Avoid engaging in excessive conversation in person's presence. Learn to remain quiet.

When it's time to speak, be careful to select your words and don't rush to pour out your words.

You can convince someone that you're a secret-keeper and that you can manage any scenario.

The habit of saying "I apologize" even though you've done nothing wrong.

If you've just been hurt someone or need to confront the person with your own wisdom be sure to practice the way you'll address it, and the tone you use.

Slow to speak and listen quickly.

Pay attention to the mood and mood before you speak your mind.

The act of praying to God regarding the heart of the person toward you is also employing powerful words in indirect ways.

Do not play serious issues by putting a smile on your face when you are in someone's presence. There's time for everything.

Always pay attention to the reactions and look of your face whenever you use specific words. This will allow you to identify which words you need to remove or similar ones you could use in the event of a positive reaction.

If you are required to begin any conversation with your manager or supervisor, take your time to observe the mood and environment. You should ask permission before beginning.

Your words should be so powerful that when you leave the message will ring within the heart of the recipient.

Sometimes, it is necessary to be quiet and say nothing in order for peace to rule. It is also a strength of words. It is a sign of the ability to control your emotions.

Don't make a report about a person who is difficult to someone else. This could lead to a worsening of the situation. One way to avoid it is to inform an individual who is struggling to him or her.

There are many methods to make use of word power to manage the difficult person.

Chapter 20: The Guilt Tripper

The act of guilt tripping is among that of the most manipulative methods that people employ to obtain what they need. If someone can in making you feel guilty, it's possible to obtain almost everything you want from them. But, you should not think about making excuses for guilt-tripping others because this method could actually cause stress for others and you could be able to lose their respect.

Be aware of the signs that tell you something is wrong.

The most effective strategies to deal with people who are prone to using the guilt trips is to end it in the beginning. Don't allow yourself to be lured into others' guilt trips. You can avoid this by knowing how to identify people who guilt-trips on you. When someone begins talking about you using the words"If you were more reliable, you would then you could ..."or"If you really love me," you should ...", be cautious as the person who is talking to you could be trying to convince you to join one of his guilt-trips. In these phrases you will find that the person trying to get you what they would like for you to follow. Guilt trippers are also known to create a guilt-trip by telling you exactly what they should not do. For instance,"I realized that what I heard was not true. I'm sure you'll never begin a new project without talking to my first." When you make that line of reasoning the person who made it has clearly stated what he's asking you to do, which is to talk about all projects with him before beginning any project.

The guilt should be transferred to the person who did it

If someone is making you feel guilty to achieve his goals If you feel guilty, you can employ the same strategy on him to ensure that he can understand the consequences of his behavior. If someone is trying to manipulate you with guilt, you can react by telling him that they aren't caring about the way you behave, and expressing appreciation or gratitude for your attitude toward him. If you can accomplish this, you'll be able stop your obligation to meet the obligation the other person is trying to impose on you. For example, if someone in your circle tells you that you don't appear to be interested in the work to help him, he can tell you that they are doing their best to assist you, say that you truly take care of him and they don't acknowledge how much you value your efforts. If he responds that he is grateful for your help then you can tell him to say that the same is true as you and are grateful for the efforts he has put into it.

Reducing guilt trippers' hold on you

If a guilt-tripper tries to trick you into believing that he is making suggestions that do not seem to have any significance to you, don't trust his tricks. You may choose to respond with a swift response that stops the manipulation right away. A good example of a guilt-trip assertion is:"It okay. You just need to select X to take part in the project, while I tidy up the mess that he left in this incomplete project. Don't be worried about me, I'm fine."You can stop the manipulative part by saying,"That's fantastic! I'm very happy to hear that you're happy with the project you've been working on. I really appreciate that Thank you!"

Take the assumption statement from your Assumption statements typically begin with"I guess"or"I wish"or"I think". There are a few examples "I hope the management realizes the difficulty it will be for me to keep working on this task"or"I think I'll be added to the group of individuals who can be considered for promotion as I've been the one who has the greatest contribution in the group this season." Guilt trippers enjoy using assumptions since they're not really asking questions, which they are not able to ask because it makes them to feel that they're losing their control. If you're dealing with an honest person they will inquire in order to understand the truth about what you're doing, and continue an interaction in accordance with the information you share. An individual who is guilt-tripping On the other hand is likely to simply offer his own assumptions about the actions you're taking to enable him to influence your behavior. He will want that you do the things he thinks that you'll do instead of listening to the things you really intend to accomplish. Here's how to avoid assumptions from you:

Guilt Tripper:"I want to be on the list of candidates for promotion because I've been the greatest contributor in the group this season."

You:"The Management team is going to take this decision based upon corporate policies."

Guilt Tripper:"I believe you will not back me, and won't recommend my promotion."

You:"You know that I highly recommend all my subordinates that have outstanding performance. Your qualifications will be scrutinized by my management staff to determine whether you qualify for promotion."

Guilt Tripper:"If you don't believe that my performance won't allow me to be promoted I don't think you have to bother providing me with recommendations."

You:"I am happy that you have a good understanding of the policies of the company in regard to promotions."

Don't join an unrepentant guilt-tripper while he plays mind games with others

Some guilt-trippers do not believe that they're forcing their will upon you. Therefore, they'll use others as a source of authority. If they want you to perform something, they'll inform you that they have an uncle or other experienced person with success who's completed the same thing previously with good results. A guilt-tripper can employ this method when he suspects that you're not responding to the manipulative tactics they are using.

Following our previous example, the guilt tripping person may continue with his agenda, claiming that the boss of the department in question believes that he's ripe to be promoted and that his performance are superior to the outputs of other people within the company. When he says this, the guilt-tripper gives up the responsibility for making statements that they really want to be hearing. It is possible to cut off the deceit by saying:"I didn't know that the boss in the opposite department aware of every aspect that you're doing. I believe that I must meet with her and discuss this issue with her."

Beware of being confronted with guilt-trippers

You must be careful when dealing with guilt-trippers. They usually use tricks as well as mind games, to cause conflict or disputes against you when they don't receive what they want. If a guilt tripper suspects that you're not heeding to his hints and tricks, he'll use arguments and conflict to gain power over you. The guilt-tripper may use aggressive statements in the hope of angering you, so you'll get into an dispute with him. He could say to you,"You have never been a friend to me. Your efforts are always ignored. You are not aware of me." In lieu of getting into a heated debate with the guilt-tripper, you can just reply by saying a"no"and then provide factual facts. React calmly and rationally the guilt-tripper. Don't provoke an argument by smiling or responding in a negative manner. Make sure to keep your replies friendly and easy.

Dodge the self-pity

If you listen to someone who is a guilt-tripper say that everything is unfair to him and that the person is doing nothing wrong the truth is that he's trying to gain your sympathy to use it later to his own benefit. If you fall for his trap, the guilt-tripper will be influenced by his inability to seek any kind of assistance from you, including financial and emotional support. Be wary of words or attitudes that suggest to you"Oh it's you, the only person I can truly rely on"or"You can be my only one who respects me". If your colleague begins to play his self-pity plan on you, show compassion however, be aware that you don't really wish to be completely obligated to him. You can respond with"You know that's not the case. You can reach out to the HR manager or directly to the department head if you're having any questions or concerns,"or"I am sure that both x and y will be open to hearing from your concerns and offer assistance in whatever way you need."

Beware of those who alter and change facts to make them appear more attractive.

They generally are likely to use lies in order to gain the things they need from their peers. This is often seen in the workplace , since they want their coworkers on their side or appear good before higher authority. If you suspect that you've been told inaccurate information, it is best to seek clarification. Be honest when you say that this isn't what you are remembering and that you want to gain a better understanding of the situation Be courteous and respectful. You can simply say that you would like clarification as you are unclear. Ask questions that are basic to the agreement you've made and the way in which you believe the other party believes that it was made. Utilize the guilt tripper's responses to clarify the truth. Be wary of people who appear to have "selective memories" because they are a different method of manipulating and controlling other people. People who use selective memory to get out of the responsibilities they don't want to undertake and yet recall the duties they wish to fulfill.

Don't fall victim of guilt-trippers whom use"love" to bargain. means to negotiate

Certain guilt trippers use the following phrases to influence you to give them what you want:"Because you are sure I am in love with you, please do this, this, in my honor ..."or"I believe that you truly appreciate me, so do this and and that ..."This kind of manipulation is often used in relationships and friendships , but it is able to be modified somewhat to function in a workplace atmosphere. The guilt trippers who display these types of behavior usually would like you to feel obliged. Do not worry, you can stop those who are close to you from manipulating the feelings of love and affection for them by explaining the ways that your actions show how much you cherish them. You will improve your outcomes by showing more compassion and telling your loved ones how much you value their affection and concern for you too. When a subordinate demands you to do something in order to show that you care about his well-being, you can respond that you truly consider his welfare a priority and that's the reason you're doing what it is that you're doing. Do not be shy about listing the positive things you offer your subordinates.

Find out the fake ailments that guilt trippers are known to create

It's a shame that guilt-trippers even go as far as making use of illness as a tool to manipulate others. Certain guilt-trippers use minor ailments and signs to win the sympathy of others however, they actually suffer with Munchausen's Syndrome or Factitious Disorder. They make up their illness by deliberately creating fake symptoms and exaggerated signs to get what they desire. Some guilt-trippers are doing this to avoid having to fulfill their obligations, and also to allow more time to enjoy relaxation and leisure and others do it in order to maximize their health advantages. However, some are simply lazy and constantly want others to complete their jobs for them.

If you observe that a friend or subordinate has a habit of engaging in this type of behavior You should start thinking about whether he truly needs medical assistance from a psychologist, or psychiatrist since he could have Factitious Disorder. If someone else does indeed suffer from Factitious Disorder, it is best to be cautious about making judgments. Most people develop the disorder in response to stress, until it has become a problem behaviour. To show compassion to someone else, you could offer your suggestion to let the person seeking help get a mental health specialist to help him deal in overcoming his anxieties and worries however, you should be cautious regarding the person's fake illness.

Do not be fooled by guilt trippers that manipulate your emotions by triggering emotional anger

Some guilt trippers make use of screaming, sadness crying and other kinds of emotions to gain their desired outcomes from others. It is common among adolescents and young children who utilize emotional outbursts to influence their parents and others to get what they desire. If you find that a colleague or subordinate is constantly using his emotions to persuade you to comply with the things he demands and you are unable to resist, be firm when saying no. However, you must remain at peace and respectful. It is possible to show your compassion by suggesting to the other person seek assistance by a mental health professional who can assist him to deal with his emotions.

Be aware of your own self.
If you're dealing with someone who is a guilt-tripper It is important to learn to be aware of your self to determine your own feelings and thoughts concerning the matter. You must determine if the behavior of the other person make you feel oppressed, pressured and pressured to submit to the desires of the other but

which you don't wish to do so. Your own feelings and thoughts to lead you to where you would like you and the guilt-tripper to be.

Chapter 21: Discover To Effectively Communicate

There aren't many people born with powerful problem-solving skills. But that doesn't mean you won't be able to develop these skills. In fact, all through our lives, it's crucial to make some time each and every day in order to develop into an improved problem solver.

The reason is because people who have excellent problem-solving skills are able to work with others as well. They also make excellent leaders, enjoy better relationships with others as well as better co-operation from their team members and, most importantly they earn the respect of those who surrounds them.

Now, the question is how can you become a superb problem-solver?

To begin, you must to be able to differentiate the problem and the individual. This way, you'll be capable of being soft with people you're dealing and tough in dealing with the problem.

A conversation, for instance, could be like this:

"I am wishing for two of us to have a conversation however I'm not able do it when you're angered. We can either keep our cool and remain relaxed about the situation or we could take a break for a few minutes and then return to discuss this issue later. It's your choice."

Alternatively, try this:

"I thank you for taking on such a huge role for me the past couple of days. But, you're not yet ahead with your tasks. I'd like to speak with you about ways to make it easier for you to complete your work within the timeframe you promised."

Keep in mind that when we're soft with those we deal with they are more willing to listen to our opinions. If individuals are open to their opinions, they're likely to get better and perform better next time around.

What do you'd like to see be the case? Do you not want your sloppy student to stop earning Fs on every test and at a minimum, get Cs on the following time?

If you're ever dealing with someone, keep in mind this phrase: "firm on the issue Soft to the individual."

Chapter 22: How To Manage An Uncomfortable Boss And Be Able To Keep Your Job

Certain bosses are great to work with. While they may require you to put in the hours however, they also have reasonable demands and give you the flexibility to achieve the right balance between your work and personal life. Other bosses, however, can be excessively demanding, and frequently make unrealistic expectations that could cause you to become agitated. If you are someone who belongs to the latter category then you must come up with a method to deal with your boss in a professional and reasonable manner.

Effective Communication Skills

One of the most important actions you can take when working under a demanding boss is to develop the power of communication. If you are the kind of person who will give you half-instructions or make changes at the end of a project, make sure you bring an eraser for every meeting you attend with them. Write down any directions they give you. Before leaving their premises take the time to repeat the instructions you wrote down. This accomplishes two things. It allows your boss the capability to modify the instructions prior to you beginning working on the task. Additionally, it lets it appear that you're dedicated and diligent to following the directions to the letter. It is advisable to communicate with your boss regarding the progress of your project several times to make sure that the work you do is up to requirements.

Set Limits

It is essential to know the rights you have as a professional and set limits on your working hours and your free time. If you are not in a position in which you must be on call, it's not reasonable or proper for your boss to contact you on your off hours regarding workplace-related issues. The calls should be routed to voice messages. Pay attention to the messages and then send a short SMS message to the boss telling him that you're out of pocket. You can talk to them about it early and before the day you are scheduled to work. Beware of being enticed into working late, whenever you can. Be aware that once you've established a pattern of working late or on weekends, it can become a routine.

Keep Your the distance

It is essential to keep a the distance to your supervisor as far as is possible. This is a person you have to work with and get orders from, however this doesn't mean you have to be with him all the all the time. You can lessen your irritation with the person you work with and reduce your blood pressure by doing your work on your own whenever you can. Be sure to avoid any other activities that involve the boss out of work. If you're allowed to work at home as often as feasible. Follow the steps you have to do to maintain the job you have and to not appear aloof. It is, however, beneficial when you are dealing with someone who has a negative effect on you.

Most people encounter a difficult boss at some point or another. The way you manage your relationship with the person can affect your mental health and the ability to stay in your job. Use these tips to more efficiently manage your challenging boss.

Chapter 23: Deal With The Difficult Person, And Use "I" Statements

This must be the most difficult of the strategies for dealing with people who are difficult. There is nothing more unpleasant than confrontation. When we consider confrontation, we usually imagine going towards someone and saying, "You are really a rude person, so why do you feel so mean to me? I have never done anything wrong against you." This isn't the type of confrontation we'd like to engage in with someone who is difficult, especially in our workplace or with our neighbors.

There are many different approaches to deal with the problem both of you are facing. The first is to talk about the family. A good example of having an interaction with someone you cherish is having a conversation with that person in a private space with no one else in the vicinity. Begin the conversation by saying something positive.

"Grandpa I know you am the most devoted person on earth I am aware that you're very isolated without Grandma. I am sure that arthritis causes pain everywhere. "I am feeling" awful when you say that. What can I help you so you're not feeling so down? Do I have to take an appointment with a doctor and see what sort of medicine or herb that can help you not be in suffering? I don't like seeing you suffering."

There's always something you could assist the person, but remember to make use of "I" phrases. This will take the accusation curve off of phrases. It doesn't make the person who is accused in a defensive position. It's possible that the person doesn't know that they're creating this kind of impact on other people.

We also have neighbors and this one is likely to be more challenging to handle. Most of the time, kindness and words of encouragement will be helpful. However, if they don't, an informal meeting could help to kick off the process. Bring a platter with cookies, and then invite yourself to join by telling them you'd like to discuss with them about something significant to you.

Begin by making a positive statement for example, "Your yard is so beautiful and your flowers are gorgeous to look at and make our backyard smell so nice. Thanks for being such a kind neighbor. I'd like to repay the favor and become a good neighbor for you, too. What is the best thing I could do to make it happen? Are we loud enough? Do we interfere with your child's practice with the trumpet? Feel free to let me know if we're irritating anyone in some way. We're trying to become the most pleasant neighbor we could be. We can help to any extent?" More than that There aren't any other things you can make or say. You've to be willing to share your story. The ball is in his yard right now!

Then, we are back in the office. We've tried the usual thread, we've experimented with positive words, seemingly random act of kindness. There is a third possibility to explore.

If the person who is difficult for you is your boss and all the actions you've done haven't made any impact on how your boss is treating you, then you've got several options. (1) You should visit the Human Resources Department and speak to the director, not the secretary. Discuss your experience with the director and pray that things will improve. (2) If your boss's behavior is sexual or emotional harassment talk to an attorney (especially in the event that you've spoken with H.R. and nothing is done) Or (3) You may ask to be transferred to a different department, or start seeking out a new job. Conversations are not always successful when you attempt to speak to an employee who is unprofessional.

If, for instance, the troublesome person is a colleague you must collaborate with each day You will have to request to talk with this individual in private. Always begin the conversation with a positive attitude. "You are the most efficient scheduler I've ever had the pleasure of working with. I appreciate the way you manage my demands," then add the "I" assertions. "I find myself annoyed when I deliver documents on your table. Sometimes I feel that you may be angry at me. Do I do that is offensive to you? Is there a better approach for me to contact you with concerns or questions? Is there a better day to make this request? I'd like to assist in any way I can to help make our relationship stronger. Do you have any suggestions to help me?"

Utilizing the "I" phrases keeps the person who is struggling from getting in a defensive mode. It's true that you're the only one among your two that takes the time to resolve the issue or improve them. This exposes the behaviour into the view of the opposite party without accusing them for being disrespectful. It does bring it to the attention of the other person. In this moment it's time to move to the next step.

Chapter 24: Discussion About Them

The people who have difficulty deal with things differently. Instead of discussing the issue and figuring out how to solve it they are quick to pinpoint the problem. This is exactly why they make them difficult to tackle as it doesn't solve anything.

The reason these people do it is because they wish for you to feel uncomfortable. They want you to feel down about yourself. When you feel that way, they will are able to feel better in themselves and relieve themselves of of their own fears.

There are many of them every day, and more frequently at work. The best approach to approach them is to stay away from being defensive. When you're in a defensive mood, people will examine your actions. When you let others take advantage of you, you are giving them authority over you.

The fastest and most effective method to prevent this from happening is to focus the spotlight back to them. Instead of letting yourself become the subject of the conversation, try to redirect the conversation to them.

For instance, the conversation might go as follows:

Difficult People: "What you're doing isn't anything like what I told you to accomplish."

Your: "Did you ever stop to consider what you would like me to accomplish?"

Difficult People: "You're just so stupid. What do you think?"

Yousay "Keep going with it" and you'll never be able to have someone working for you for a long time. I'm sure you do not wish to do to do that. Let me know what you'd like to achieve and I'll take care of it for you. If you aren't able to, I'll be happy to take it on."

As you will observe, this isn't an option to be used defensively when doing things. More of an aggressive method that allows you to maintain an open mind regarding issues.

If you keep the spotlight on the problematic person helps reduce their negativity and consequently, minimize their influence on you.

Chapter 25: Easy Rules Of Dealing With Difficult People

When you deal with people who can be difficult your reputation can be at risk. What you say can impact your reputation. Your mental and emotional well-being could be affected too. Here are a few simple guidelines to remember whenever you meet people who are difficult to get along with.

Make sure you think before you act

Before you reply or take action consider it for a second and try to anticipate the probable outcome of response. This way you'll avoid uncomfortable situations. If you act abruptly and without thinking about it, you might be faced with the consequences that could occur. Don't take on this burden. When you present an intelligent and thoughtful response in either a verbal or your actions, you are able to influence the other person thinking too.

Stay cool

Always remain calm regardless of how the reaction of the other person and don't allow them to become a source of stress. There is no way to keep your temper in check unless you allow them to. Being calm and cool can deter those around you as they're likely to seek an argument. It also allows you to consider the best option for you. There have been instances of people losing their cool in traffic and then do an unwise thing. There will surely be individuals who will test your patience, but you shouldn't let your temper get out of control.

Don't be offended.

When you meet a challenging person, always remember that what they're saying outwardly is an expression of their inner tension. It's not about them or anything, it's just about the person. A person may be experiencing difficult times in their life and they are likely to be angry. The best way to deal with this is understand their situation and work with them to overcome the problem that is causing them to be angry in a different approach. If someone can see that you care about them and feel empathy for them, they will be able to shift their perspective towards you.

Search within

In certain situations it is possible for someone to become difficult because of your behavior or attitude. Before you criticize or criticize, you should first look inside to determine whether your behavior is correct. It is a difficult thing to achieve since people think they're not at fault. You may have offended someone unintentionally. If you realize that you could be the source of the different attitudes you're encountering from people around you Make it a priority to address the issue. If you resolve the issue quickly it will prevent any accumulation of anger and bitterness.

Be aware of your goals

Every activity we engage in, there is something we wish to accomplish even in our conversations. When you are aware of the goal you are aiming for then you can rise above other small-minded concerns that are often the reason for difficult interactions with other people. You don't want to be retributive nor do you want to do harm to someone else.

Listen actively

The majority of disagreements we encounter result from a an inability to listen. If people had the skills of active listening, the majority of conflicts could be prevented. Pay attention with the intent to be able to understand, not to respond. Uncertainties can lead to conflicts that can create a situation where working with people is very difficult. Once you understand the meaning of the other person's words through spoken and non-verbal communication and you're in a position to respond appropriately. It is not necessary to agree with the other person, but being able to understand their perspective can go a long way towards improving relationships.

Chapter 26: How To Handle Employees Who Are Difficult To Deal With

We're pleased to introduce the second section of this guide on managing employees who are difficult; in this chapter we'll be talking about various scenarios for personnel that you could face in your career as a manager. If you're dealing with a lazy employee an employee who is toxic and absenteeism, those who want to raise their pay or an employee with a possible drug abuse issue There's help and guidance in this book.

As I mentioned earlier managing personnel issues is among the most challenging tasks you'll need to complete, which is why you must be aware and current on the most recent policies and managerial thinking. The suggestions in this section were drawn from my personal experience in management as well as countless discussions with colleagues across the nation.

Before we discuss our first employee problem scenario It's important to discuss the reasons that some employees appear to be destined to make your life difficult.

The first thing to be aware of when dealing with difficult employees is that they're often in this state because their behavior has been a success for them and has not been dealt with at any point in time. It is likely that through engaging in a shrewd manner, defying accountability or simply being lazy and out the employee has gotten outcomes in the past, regardless of whether they have more work or a sense of power or the belief that they are able to do whatever they want and be able to get out of it. This is something you must take on. It's like an infant; if an infant knows that it's possible to get attention by crying and will repeat the process every time until someone interrupts the cycle.

In some instances it is possible that the employee's behavior might not be truly intentional. It could be due to ignorance of the situation, fear, confusion, or even a inability to motivate. Your role as a supervisor is to determine the root of the behaviour issue in the best way you can and take appropriate action.

If you're being a part of someone else's team and the behavior was not addressed, or was a behavior you had previously disapproved of through the lack of action or action, it isn't a matter of. The time to act is now. If you have employee's behavior, you are the only one to be required to change the pattern of conduct they've been practicing for years.

You could find that the majority of your time managing people is being consumed by only 10 percent or less of the employees. You must become as effective as possible with the tenth percent of your workforce in order to give your time to devote to the remaining 90 percent. As a line supervisor, it is your responsibility to ensure that every employee is aware of what the business - and you - expect of them and it's their duty to fulfill the expectations of the company.

It's also important to realize that all employees aren't always easy as we all have access to moods, emotions , and stress. The employees who are consistently challenging, but are not willing to make changes are ones you'll need to tackle. They are the most difficult employees.

It's not always the case that they're your most effective or valuable members of your staff. On contrary the fact that someone could be a good employee in a variety of ways, does not mean they are get away with it when they constantly take credit for others' work or putting others down, or being aggressive towards everyone else in their vicinity.

If you want to change the offending behavior to a positive one, you need to take action swiftly and decisively. Do not ignore it simply as it's more convenient to ignore it and it doesn't help anyone and the person who is causing offence staff included.

One fact is important to keep on your mind all the time and you'll discover it allows you to have an objective look at situations which is there is no absolute necessity for anyone. Everyone is able to be replaced, even you! Every manager has employed staff members they did not want to lose that they thought that the company would lose and struggle with leaving. It may be because they excelled in their field or they were knowledgeable that no one else did. Guess what? The company was able to survive! It could be a time of change, but people as well as teams are adaptable and there is no one who is unassailable. Don't believe to believe that someone is valuable enough to be lost... it's not true. Be aware of that every day allows you to be more proactive.

The information contained within this field is created with one purpose in mind, namely fixing the issue and making the employee a satisfied and productive employee in your organization. You are responsible to every employee who works for you to offer them the opportunity to change their behavior before taking more drastic steps.

It might require several meetings and discussion, or even a confrontation to accomplish this however, the outcomes might be worthwhile at the end. A few years ago, I had one employee who was unprofessional and whose behavior caused working with her to be extremely difficult. I was close to removing her from the company many times, but in final, I fought. This person is now an employee and is incredibly proficient at what she does. She says that our time together was the most important moment in her life, when she removed herself from the negative and anger that was triggered by a bad childhood and focused on the future.

These stories of success are what make the effort involved in managing employees with issues worth it. But, there will occur instances when the outcomes aren't as positive. It is crucial to recognize the times when you're not in your comfort zone or can't resolve the issue on your own. Certain employees might have mental problems or addictions aren't able to overcome The best option for hanging on to those employees is to seek out professional help.

It is also essential to be aware of when things have become too extreme for an employee to remain within your organization In this case, you might need to look at terminating the employee. In all instances, regardless of the reason the fundamental rules for termination should be followed , as described within our section on disciplining employees.

Let's say for the moment that things aren't too serious yet, and concentrate on providing the tools to change problematic behavior. Let's address one of our employees...

Chapter 27: Different Types Of Difficult People

There are many kinds of people who are difficult:

A Possible Person

A possible friend or colleague struggles to decide on their decision. They usually avoid making choices due to the fear of not pleasing you. An excellent example is when you watch an entertainment with your members of your group and start an argument about who dies first in the film. If you decide to cast the majority vote, and your friend could be the tiebreaker, they would not take part in a vote based on the fact that the resulting actions of one of the two of you.

Another characteristic of a possible friend is that they tends to delay decisions in the hopes of finding a better solution. This can be a challenge since the outcomes could affect your life directly. One good example is a situation where you and your spouse have been planning your wedding, and you conduct interviews with a couple of wedding planners. After that, you narrow them down and decide on two names you think will be the best to go with You then give your partner to select which one to select. As a naive person, your fiancee may put off the decision and wait until she misses out on both planners when they are booked.

Super Agreeable

Another type of hard-working people is the one who is super-agreeable. These people tend to accept every word you have to say. They will always be in your corner until you demand actions from them. Then , they move on and disappoint you. One good example is planning to become weight loss buddies with a person you know If the friend is the super friendly person, he or she, will be willing to go to the gym with you, and could even help to find a great gym. However, when it comes time to commit to workout and you are not able to keep up with your friend, they abandon you.

These types of people have to get along with everyone they say, pretend to like and respect everyone, and make false promises that they can't make.

Complainers

People like this can be difficult to deal with because they be critical of all you do since they perceive the world as hostile and unfair environment. When you encounter this kind of person, you'll always be greeted with complaints. It can be difficult to spot them since they cover up their grievances in actual issues. The result is that you turn into a defensive individual anytime you're around that person due to the continuous blame that the person places on you.

One of the most common traits among complainants is their perceived powerlessness when it comes to their area of complaint. The main goal of complainers is to make a complaint, but they shy away from solving problems.

The Aggressive Type

These kinds of people typically bullies who harass and harass you. They usually believe that you are an insignificant victim and are entitled to the treatment they're giving you. These kinds of people are usually motivated when you display indicators of vulnerability. They can be classified into twogroups:

1. There are some who will attack individuals by pointing out and yelling at you in a rage when discussing an entirely different subject than the idea of a project or idea.

2. And then there are people who are strongly convinced of what you're supposed to think and behave. They believe that what they do and think about how you should act and think. They typically make rude comments and sharp sarcasm.

The Know-It-All

The"know it all" person falls into two types.

1. The experts: The expert is knowledgeable and efficient. They are usually overflowing with "themselves" and generally act superior. They also make use of their knowledge for making you look

foolish. They're intolerant of others' ideas that they think are insignificant, and they will never seek your assistance.

2. The uninformed The person who is not fully informed will argue with you simply because they have only a little knowledge of a specific area. This kind of person has a difficult time working with due to the fact that they don't listen to other people's opinions and views.

Conclusion

I recall one day specifically when I'd been so upset by someone who made me feel totally out of character. What was the reason I allowed the person to bother me so much where it I was angry? What gave this person the ability to influence me in this manner? I took some deep breaths and I made the decision to conduct a A LOT of research! After doing my research I reached this conclusion. If anyone could cause me to be angry and hurt this deeply, then it was something I had to address. I was required to take responsibility for myself. How can I allow other people to change my attitude due to the fact that they are accustomed to being difficult? It became for me that tough people are the way they are, and I shouldn't give in to their despair, Therefore, I must not let others alter my mood.

I can't control the actions of others However, I can however manage my feelings. I needed to ask myself what I was doing allowing anyone else to ruin my day simply because they are unhappy? In the instances when I was in the midst of a momentary mess in my life, I have never taken my problems out on other people because it wasn't right. Understanding this is how difficult people have altered my life for the better! Instead of allowing people to approach me with their unfounded motives I am always prepared to shine my light and I will never stop shining my light! Don't let anyone block your happiness ever! Your happiness is the sunshine you have! Keep pushing forward with your personal growth and people can be inspired by the attitude throughout the process. Additionally, I encourage you to read everything you can on this subject to gain a the feeling of being empowered in this field. I believe that no resource can provide all the answers, so do your research as thoroughly possible. Additionally, you will never be knowledgeable enough, and there's always the possibility of improvement.

I hope that this book was useful in helping you know the four major kinds of people who are difficult and the best way to handle each one effectively. I also hope you've learned something useful about your sun. Next step, integrate the lessons you've discovered and feel confident with in your daily interactions and commit to strengthen your relations with others even those who are difficult and challenging.

www.ingramcontent.com/pod-product-compliance
Lightning Source LLC
Chambersburg PA
CBHW071838080526
44589CB00012B/1035